# Why is there Money?

For Daniel and Wendy,
Diana, Oren, Lior and Aviv

# Why is there Money?

Walrasian General Equilibrium Foundations
of Monetary Theory

Ross M. Starr

*University of California, San Diego, USA*

**Edward Elgar**

Cheltenham, UK • Northampton, MA, USA

Published by
Edward Elgar Publishing Limited
The Lypiatts
15 Lansdown Road
Cheltenham
Glos GL50 2JA
UK

Edward Elgar Publishing, Inc.
William Pratt House
9 Dewey Court
Northampton
Massachusetts 01060
USA


A catalogue record for this book
is available from the British Library


Library of Congress Control Number: 2011936344

ISBN 978 1 84844 856 8 (cased)

Typeset by Servis Filmsetting Ltd, Stockport, Cheshire
Printed and bound by MPG Books Group, UK

# Contents

# Tables

# Acknowledgements

The author and publisher wish to thank the following who have kindly given permission for the use of copyright material.

Cambridge University Press for article R. Starr and M. Stinchcombe, 'Exchange in a network of trading posts', in Graciela Chichilnisky (ed.), *Markets, Information and Uncertainty* (1999) © Graciela Chichilnisky, published by Cambridge University Press.

Elsevier for article R. Starr, 'Mengerian saleableness and commodity money in a Walrasian trading post example', *Economics Letters*, **100** (2008), pp. 35–8; for article R. Starr, 'Commodity money equilibrium in a convex trading post economy with transaction costs', *Journal of Mathematical Economics*, 2008, **44**, pp. 1413–27; and for article R. Starr, 'The Jevons double coincidence condition and local uniqueness of money: an example', *Journal of Mathematical Economics*, 2010, **46**, pp. 786–92.

Springer Science+Business Media B.V. for article (including diagram) R. Starr, 'Why is there money? Endogenous derivation of "money" as the most liquid asset: a class of examples', *Economic Theory*, 2003, **21** (2–3), March, pp. 455–74; and for article (including diagram) R. Starr, 'Existence and uniqueness of "money" in general equilibrium: natural monopoly in the most liquid asset', in *Assets, Beliefs, and Equilibria in Economic Dynamics*, edited by C.D. Aliprantis, K.J. Arrow, P. Hammond, F. Kubler, H.-M. Wu and N.C. Yannelis, Heidelberg: BertelsmanSpringer, 2004.

Every effort has been made to trace all the copyright holders but if any have been inadvertently overlooked the publisher will be pleased to make the necessary arrangements at the first opportunity.

# Introduction: why is there no money?

[An] important and difficult question . . . [is] not answered by the approach
taken here: the integration of money in the theory of value . . .

Gerard Debreu, *Theory of Value* (1959)

## A CHALLENGE

During the 1970s at Yale's Cowles Foundation, the most serious scientific
conversations took place in the coffee lounge. As a junior colleague then
in the company of leading monetary economists James Tobin, William
Brainard and Henry Wallich, I remember a discussion of inflation. One
colleague said 'Well, Herb Scarf [a general equilibrium theorist] says . . . .'
Bill Brainard replied, 'But Herb can only give you relative prices. He
doesn't have a monetary model'. Indeed, it was generally viewed then as
impossible to derive a monetary theory from the Arrow—Debreu general
equilibrium model. Brainard's remark echoed decades of tradition as
Hicks (1935) and Tobin (1961) had challenged microeconomic theory to
present a sound account of money.

## THE RESPONSE

Professor Brainard's reply was an (almost) fully accurate description of
the state of monetary theory embodied in the prevailing Arrow—Debreu
general equilibrium model. But I hoped things were changing for the better.
I had personally been trying to incorporate money in the Arrow—Debreu
model and there had been progress elsewhere. Duncan Foley and I had
discussed Foley (1970) prior to publication — that paper seemed a great
start. Frank Hahn had presented Hahn (1971) in 1969 at the Econometric
Society meeting. By 1973 we had Starrett (1973) which included 'money'
in the title.

These essays presented a model of general equilibrium with transaction costs so that the price space was augmented to include bid and ask
prices. It seemed only a quick step to identify 'money' as the low transaction cost instrument (as Starrett had done). Then we would surely

have a fully monetized Arrow–Debreu model. Why the focus on this general equilibrium model? Professor Hugo Sonnenschein remarked: 'The Arrow–Debreu model, as communicated in *Theory of Value* . . . quickly became the standard model of price theory. It is the "benchmark" model'. But even Hahn (1982, p. 1) who had made so much progress was not sanguine: 'The . . . challenge that . . . money poses to the theorist is this: the best developed model of the economy cannot find room for it. The best developed model is, of course, the Arrow–Debreu version of a Walrasian general equilibrium'.

What puzzles must a price-theoretic fundamental model of money resolve?

- Trade is monetary. One side of almost all transactions is the economy's common medium of exchange.
- Money is (virtually) unique. Though money differs among economies, almost all the transactions in most places most of the time use a single common medium of exchange.
- Even transactions suitable for barter resolution, displaying a double coincidence of wants, are transacted with money.
- Money is government-issued fiat money, trading at a positive value though it conveys directly no utility or production.

This volume attempts satisfactorily to solve these puzzles using the standard tools of price and general equilibrium theory.

## THE IMPOSSIBLE TAKES A LITTLE LONGER

We have been waiting four decades for general equilibrium theory to completely fulfill the promise of Foley (1970) and Hahn (1971), giving us an Arrow–Debreu theory of money. It has not quite happened. Part of the difficulty is that money takes a variety of forms and fulfills a multiplicity of functions: medium of exchange, store of value, unit of account. The other is that the Arrow–Debreu model sets a very high standard of parsimonious structure: assume as little as possible,[1] and infer results as much as possible. So the model of this volume makes just two additions to the Arrow–Debreu model. Exchange is a resource-using activity; the budget constraint applies not merely to the sum of all trades but to each transaction separately. This volume concentrates on the medium of exchange function – something completely absent from the classic Arrow–Debreu model. In that model, trade is costless and instantaneous, subject to a single grand budget constraint. Here, exchange is a resource-using activity with a requirement that payment be made for acquisitions at each of many separate transactions, thus giving rise to a role for a carrier of value between trades.

## PLAN OF THIS VOLUME[2]

Chapter 1 introduces the array of issues and a historical overview of the monetary theory literature dealing with them. This is a topic that can seem very diffuse, so the closing section gives a price theory perspective on the issues treated in the remainder of the volume — a cheat sheet for the microeconomic theorist. Chapter 2 presents an overview of the Arrow–Debreu general equilibrium model that is the focus of so much attention above. It represents the common classroom exercise of thinking through the implications of an economy operating without money.

Chapter 3 presents the real workhorse of this volume, the trading post model. The model posits separate trading arrangements for each pair of commodities that may trade for one another. If there are $N$ commodities in the economy, there are $\frac{1}{2}N(N - 1)$ distinct trading posts where exchange may take place. Chapter 4 presents the first tentative step at fulfillment of the plan, an example of a linear economy with active trade in a trading post model where the price system guides all trade to use the low transaction cost instrument as the common medium of exchange. Chapter 5 uses the same model to demonstrate that in a linear economy, *absence* of double coincidence of wants is essential to monetization of trade.

Chapter 6 focuses on scale economies as an explanation for the uniqueness of 'money' as the medium of exchange. Scale economy — a natural monopoly — leads to a corner solution. Chapter 7 considers the dynamics of the model, converging to a unique 'money' through a dynamic tâtonnement adjustment. Chapter 8 considers the government issue of fiat 'money'. Government's power to tax can give value to a fiat instrument through government's willingness to accept it in taxes. Government's large scale, when there are scale economies in transaction costs, leads the economy to the corner solution where government-issued fiat money is the unique common medium of exchange.

Chapter 9 takes up efficiency. Trade is a resource-using activity; an efficient structure of trade will economize on its costs. Among trading post allocation mechanisms, how can we demonstrate that monetary exchange with its $N - 1$ active trading posts (out of $\frac{1}{2}N(N - 1)$ possible) is an efficient allocation mechanism? Chapter 10 tackles a foundational issue: can we explain Jevons's insistence on double coincidence of wants as a condition for barter trade as a result of transaction costs? The answer turns out to be 'yes' with a corresponding family of trading post equilibria.

Chapters 11 and 12 return to the traditional concerns of the general equilibrium theory: existence and efficiency of general equilibrium. Chapter 11 restates the trading post model in a general Arrow—Debreu style setting and shows that the conventional approach of general equilibrium modeling leads to the demonstration of existence of market equilibrium. The setting of course is quite different; instead of $N$ prices there are $N(N - 1)$ bid and ask prices at $\frac{1}{2}N(N - 1)$ separate submarkets. Chapter 12 considers the economic efficiency of monetary equilibrium. When monetary trade itself is costless, the resulting general equilibrium allocation is Pareto efficient. When non-null transaction costs affect the pattern of trade, it is easy to find examples, and a general principle, where general equilibrium allocations are not Pareto efficient (contrary to the well-known first fundamental theorem of welfare economics).

Chapters 13 and 14 conclude. Chapter 13 discusses alternative models of monetary economies. Chapter 14 summarizes the results presented here and suggests a research agenda.

## ACKNOWLEDGEMENTS

I have had useful discussions over decades regarding the research in this volume with the late Walter P. Heller, the late James Tobin, with Kenneth Arrow, Duncan Foley, Dror Goldberg, Frank Hespeler, Joseph Ostroy, Valerie Ramey, Meena Rajeev, Max Stinchcombe, Irina Telyukova, and with my students Daphne Chang, Xue Hu, Herbert Newhouse, Yu-Jung Whang, and Qiaoxi Zhang. Preparation of the manuscript of this book was facilitated by the hospitality of the Federal Reserve Bank of San Francisco and of the Stanford University Economics Department. It is a pleasure to thank my colleagues and hosts and to absolve them of responsibility for the content and any errors.

## NOTES

1. Fulfill the principle of Occam's razor.
2. This volume reflects a decade of general equilibrium modeling of a trading post economy. The issues and modeling approach of Starr (2003, 2004) appear throughout Chapters 3, 5, 6, 7, and 8. Starr (2008a) is used in Chapter 4. Chapter 9 is based on Starr and Stinchcombe (1999). Chapter 10 is based on Starr (2010). The modeling approach of Starr (2008b) is applied in Chapters 11 and 12. The treatments in this volume are intended to be more easily accessible and less formal than their journal counterparts.

# 1.   Why is there money?

This chapter focuses on three centuries of economic literature, reconciling the theory of money with the theory of value. It is challenging − on the basis of price theory − to discover the function of a medium of exchange; the rationale is transaction cost and differences in transaction cost among goods (commodity money and fiat money). Fiat money is typically an inherently useless fiduciary instrument, yet it trades at a substantial positive price. Further, though no household or firm finds it directly satisfying or productive, money is typically on one side of most transactions in the economy, the most actively traded good. These observations seem to contradict most of the theory of value. The reconciliation consists in valuing fiat money based on its acceptability in payment of taxes (an observation dating back to Smith's *Wealth of Nations*, 1776), and in deriving its function as a medium of exchange from its low transaction cost (a notion recurrent in German late 19th-century monetary theory, notably Menger's 'Origin of money', 1892).

## 1   THEORY OF MONEY AND THEORY OF VALUE

One of the oldest issues in economics is to explain the use of money, preferably in elementary terms based on the theory of value. There are contributions extending from Aristotle's *Politics*, 350 BCE and Smith's *Wealth of Nations* to the present. No economic agent can individually decide to monetize; monetary exchange should be the equilibrium outcome of interaction among optimizing agents. Money, like written language, is one of the fundamental discoveries of civilization. The superiority of monetary trade to barter explains why monetary trade is efficient but not why monetary trade is a market equilibrium. Despite the evident superiority of monetary trade, it is puzzling: monetary trade involves one party to a transaction giving up something desirable (labor, his/her production, a previous acquisition) for something useless (a fiduciary token or a commonly traded commodity for which he/she has no immediate use) in the hope of advantageously retrading it. The foundations of monetary theory should include elementary economic conditions that

*1*

allow this paradox to be sustained as an individually rational market equilibrium.

The theorems and examples of this book seek to create a parsimonious[1] model of an economy where existence of a common medium of exchange is a result of the optimizing behavior of individual firms and households. Does the price system create money? The solution proposed in this volume focuses on transaction costs and market segmentation. The monetary character of trade, use of a common medium of exchange, is shown to be an outcome of an economic general equilibrium. Markets are structured in trading posts, providing a separate possible transaction for trade of any single good in exchange for any other. For $N$ goods there are $\frac{1}{2}N(N-1)$ distinct trading opportunities. At each such transaction there is a separate budget constraint, creating demand for a carrier of value between trading posts. Monetary allocation is characterized as an outcome where most pairwise trading posts are inactive, active trade being concentrated on the $N-1$ posts trading goods for the common medium of exchange. Commodity money arises endogenously as the most liquid (lowest transaction cost) asset.

Though the use of monetary trade is virtually universal and clearly useful, understanding this institution by the fundamental principles of price theory has always been difficult. The usual classroom exercise of drawing a supply curve and a demand curve is no help at all. Even the simple general equilibrium model of an Edgeworth box (two traders, two goods) provides no help. A Robinson Crusoe model surely has no use for money. In any two-commodity model, there is essentially only one (relative) price and trade is directly of one commodity for another – and hence there is no role for money. In any two-trader model, even with many commodities, all exchange is between the two agents – and they may find it useful to have a common measure of value – but all trade is directly pairwise, so there is no role for an intermediary instrument. So what is a price theorist to do? Carl Menger (1892) firmly establishes the difficulty that the theorist faces when dealing with a successful and universal institution that defies elementary explanation. Over a century ago, Menger (p. 239) presented precisely this problem and proposed an outline of its solution, a theory of market liquidity:

> It is obvious . . . that a commodity should be given up by its owner . . . for another more useful to him. But that every[one] should be ready to exchange his goods for little metal disks apparently useless as such . . . or for documents representing [them] is . . . mysterious . . . why . . . is . . . economic man . . . ready to accept a certain kind of commodity, even if he does not need it . . . in exchange for all the goods he has brought to market[?] The problem . . . consists in giving an explanation of a general, homogeneous, course of action . . . which . . . makes

for the common interest, and yet which seems to conflict with the . . . interests of contracting individuals. [Call] goods . . . more or less saleable, according to the . . . facility with which they can be disposed of . . . at current purchasing prices or with less or more diminution . . . Men . . . exchange goods . . . for other goods . . . more saleable [which] become generally acceptable media of exchange.

'Saleability' is liquidity; a good is very saleable (liquid) if the price at which a household can sell it (the bid price) is very near the price at which it can buy (the ask price). Hence, Menger suggests that liquid goods, those with narrow spreads between bid and ask prices, become principal media of exchange, money. Liquidity creates monetization.

What characterizes a monetary economy's equilibrium, then, is that the bid–ask spread on money, the difference between the buying and selling price (or wholesale versus retail), is narrow (or zero), whereas the spread on other goods may be quite wide. Money is the good you can accept in trade without suffering a significant loss in value on trading it for another good. This property secures its position as a common medium of exchange, one that everyone willingly accepts in exchange, knowing that subsequent retrades will occur without loss.

The medium of exchange function of money is its most evident. We carry paper money around with us and use it to buy what we want. Checks and credit cards perform the same function and are alternative forms of money. The concept of a medium of exchange here is that money is the carrier of value between two interdependent transactions. The property that allows the transactions successfully to take place independently is the availability of the medium of exchange – in Martin Shubik's terms, money acts as a 'strategic decouple[r]' (1993, p. 18). Money allows separation of related sale and purchase transactions. Think, for example, of a worker who wants his wages to buy some consumer goods. First the worker provides his labor to an employer, who pays him in money. Then the worker uses the money to buy consumer goods. The worker is trading his labor for his consumption. The transactions are strongly linked: the worker will not work if he cannot acquire his desired goods in exchange; the goods will be available to the worker only in exchange for his labor. Money temporarily frees the link between the two coordinated transactions. Money appears in the middle of the trading process and dramatically simplifies it. Money is not essential to the underlying exchange of labor for goods, but it makes it much easier. The laborer's employer does not need to know or arrange for the laborer's consumption. The employer merely has to pay money. The consumer goods merchant does not need to know or arrange for the laborer's employment. The seller has merely to accept money. Thus the trade of labor for goods that the worker undertakes is separated into two far simpler elementary transactions: labor for money and money for goods.

The dismay and confusion among price theorists confronting money arises repeatedly. Hicks's (1935) principal focus was the rate of return dominance problem: why hold currency with a zero yield when there are safe assets with a positive yield? 'This, as I see it, is really the central issue in the pure theory of money. Either we have to give an explanation of the fact that people do hold money when rates of interest are positive, or we have to evade the difficulty somehow' (p. 5). As we shall see below, there are a variety of equally central issues, but Hicks provides a good test for a monetary theory – can it explain the presence of both (non-interest-bearing) money and (safe interest-bearing) bills in the same portfolio? He remarks (p. 2):

> It was marginal utility that really made sense of the theory of value; and to come to a branch of economics which does without marginal utility altogether! No wonder there are such difficulties and such differences! What is wanted is a 'marginal revolution'!
>
> That is my suggestion. But I know that it will meet with apparently crushing objections. I shall be told that the suggestion has been tried out before. It was tried by Wicksell . . . It was tried by Mises . . . The suggestion has a history, and its history is not encouraging. . . . I think we have to look . . . frictions in the face, and see if they are really so refractory after all. This will, of course, mean that we cannot allow them to go to sleep under so vague a title. The most obvious sort of friction, and undoubtedly one of the most important, is the cost of transferring assets from one form to another.

Hicks reminds us that a theory of the foundations of money necessarily requires a theory of market frictions. Conversely, a theory of perfect markets can accommodate monetary structure but necessarily cannot provide a more fundamental explanation of money's function. Tobin (1961, p. 26) comments:

> The intellectual gulf between economists' theory of the values of goods and services and their theories of the value of money is well known and periodically deplored. Twenty-five years after Hicks's eloquent call for a marginal revolution in monetary theory our students still detect that their mastery of the presumed fundamental, theoretical apparatus of economics is put to very little test in their studies of monetary economics and aggregative models. As Hicks complained, anything seems to go in a subject where propositions do not have to be grounded in someone's optimizing behavior and where shrewd but casual empiricisms and analogies to mechanics or thermodynamics take the place of inferences from utility and profit maximization. From the other side of the chasm, the student of monetary phenomena can complain that pure economic theory has never delivered the tools to build a structure of Hicks's brilliant design. The utility maximizing individual and the profit maximizing firm know everything relevant about the present and future and about the consequences of their decisions. They buy and sell, borrow and lend, save and consume, work

and play, live and let live, in a frictionless world; information, transactions, and decisions are costless. Money holdings have no place in that world, unless possession of green pieces of paper and yellow pieces of metal satisfies some ultimate miserly or numismatic taste.

The Arrow–Debreu model – developed in Arrow and Debreu (1954), Arrow (1953, 1964), Debreu (1959) – is the gold standard and benchmark of modern general equilibrium price and allocation theory. That it cannot accommodate money leaves the theory of money – as Tobin remarked – without a proper background in price theory. The prescription then from Hicks, Tobin, and Hahn, is to follow Hicks's advice, 'look the frictions in the face'. And Hicks told us almost precisely where those frictions are 'the cost of transferring assets from one form to another'. A succeeding generation of models allows us to draw on those costs for a theory of money (Foley, 1970; Hahn, 1971, 1973; Starrett, 1973).

Hahn (1982, p. 1) poses the problem for price theory in the following way:

> The most serious challenge that the existence of money poses to the theorist is this: the best developed model of the economy cannot find room for it. The best developed model is, of course, the Arrow–Debreu version of a Walrasian general equilibrium. A first, and . . . difficult . . . task is to find an alternative construction without . . . sacrificing the clarity and logical coherence . . . of Arrow–Debreu.

# 2 THE CARTALIST–METALLIST CONTROVERSY

A fiery debate spanning the 19th to the 20th century occurred between economists who argued that the value of currency is based essentially on the power of the issuing government authority (Cartalists or Chartalists) and those who argue that the value of a currency depends primarily or solely on its substance or backing (Metallists).

## 2.1 Metallism

The metallist view, well articulated below by Menger (1892), is that media of exchange arise endogenously in a trading situation, as the most convenient and liquid carriers of value between trades; cigarettes (Radford, 1945), hides, tobacco, and precious metals commonly perform this function. The choice of a unique or small number of such media reflects their inherent suitablity in terms of low transaction cost in the classic dimensions of portability, verifiability ('cognizability'), divisibility, and durability (see Jevons, 1875; Jones, 1976; Kiyotaki and Wright, 1989; Banerjee and Maskin, 1996). Money is a commodity; its monetary function is an outcome of a market equilibrium. But an extreme version of this view would be that an unbacked paper money (fiat money) trading at a positive value is logically an anomaly and practically an impossibility. Worthless paper should trade at a price of zero. Schumpeter (1954, p. 289) comments:

> theoretical metallism is untenable . . . it is not true that, as a matter of pure logic, money essentially consists in, or must be backed by, a commodity or several commodities whose exchange value as commodities are the logical basis of their value as money. The error involved consists in a confusion between the historical origin of money − which . . . may indeed be found in the fact that some commodities, being particularly salable, come to be used as the medium of exchange − and its nature or logic − which is entirely independent of the commodity character of its material.

## 2.2 'Fiat' and 'Fiat Money'

A brief digression on terminology regarding the multiple meanings of the word 'fiat' is appropriate here. Webster's Third International Unabridged Dictionary defines 'fiat' *inter alia* as 'official endorsement or sanction . . . arbitrary edict'. Meanwhile, 'fiat money' is described as 'money (as paper currency) that is not convertible into coin or specie of equivalent value and thus is dependent for its value on the decree of government'. Common usage seems now to follow a less detailed exposition: the Merriam-Webster Online Dictionary (www.merriam-webster.com/dictionary/fiat money) defines 'fiat money' without reference to government as 'money (as paper currency) not convertible into coin or specie of equivalent value'.

So there are two notions of 'fiat money': (i) inconvertible token currency promulgated by the state; and (ii) inconvertible token currency (not necessarily enforced by government). The first usage is the focus of the chartalist school; the role of government there is explicit. The second usage enters into many 20th-and 21st-century formal models − perhaps as a shorthand for the first − without explicit treatment of government.

## 2.3 Chartalism

The most prominent chartalist statement is G.F. Knapp's *Staatliche Theorie des Geldes* (1905 [1923]), 'Money is a creature of law'.

Ellis (1934, p. 16) explains: 'Chartalism is a serious theory of the social institution of money: the state causes money to be . . . Knapp's is not a fiat

theory of purchasing power, nor does it rely on fiat even to secure valu-
ableness . . . To bring this to pass, the state must [accept] money at face
value at its fiscal offices'.

In Knapp's words, 'First and foremost, [money] frees us from our
debts toward the state; for the state when emitting it, acknowledges that,
in receiving, it will accept this means of payment' (p. 52). Or as Knapp's
student Kaulla (1920, p. 55) put it, 'the note debt of the state stands
against a corresponding quantity of demands by the state which can be
unconditionally satisfied by the notes'.

## 2.4 Reconciliation

Of course, both Menger and Knapp are correct. How can we reconcile
their views? As Lerner (1947, p. 313) did:

> The modern state can make anything it chooses generally acceptable as money
> and thus establish its value quite apart from any connection, even of the most
> formal kind, with gold or with backing of any kind. It is true that a simple
> declaration that such and such is money will not do, even if backed by the
> most convincing constitutional evidence of the state's absolute sovereignty.
> But if the state is willing to accept the proposed money in payment of taxes
> and other obligations to itself the trick is done . . . On the other hand if the
> state should decline to accept some kind of money in payment of obliga-
> tions to itself, it is difficult to believe that it would retain much of its general
> acceptability.

Thus, a government with the power to tax can create the value of its fiat
money – not by announcing that its money is valuable – but rather by
accepting it for something that is valuable, forgiveness of the tax obliga-
tion. Thus as the metallists said, the state cannot create money by fiat.
And as the cartalists said, the state can create money by treating its fiat
instrument as truly valuable. Formalizing this argument in the trading
post model is the work of Chapter 8.

## 3 RESOLVING THE PROBLEM

No two-commodity model and no two-agent model can provide a foundation for the role of money in the economy. At least three agents and
three commodities are required. It is hard to picture in an economist's
usual two-dimensional illustration; it is necessarily a 'general equilibrium'
(many-commodity) problem. Smith (1776) and Wicksell (1898 [1936]) recognized this issue without fully formalizing it.

Smith (1776) commented:

> When the division of labour has been once thoroughly established, it is but
> a very small part of a man's wants which the produce of his own labour can
> supply. He supplies the far greater part of them by exchanging that surplus part
> of the produce of his own labour, which is over and above his own consump-
> tion, for such parts of the produce of other men's labour as he has occasion for.
> Every man thus lives by exchanging or becomes in some measure a merchant,
> and the society itself grows to be what is properly a commercial society. But
> when the division of labour first began to take place, this power of exchanging
> must frequently have been very much clogged and embarrassed in its opera-
> tions. One man, we shall suppose, has more of a certain commodity than he
> himself has occasion for, while another has less. The former consequently
> would be glad to dispose of, and the latter to purchase, a part of this superflu-
> ity. But if this latter should chance to have nothing that the former stands in
> need of, no exchange can be made between them. The butcher has more meat
> in his shop than he himself can consume, and the brewer and the baker would
> each of them be willing to purchase a part of it. But they have nothing to offer
> in exchange, except the different productions of their respective trades, and the
> butcher is already provided with all the bread and beer which he has immediate
> occasion for. No exchange can in this case, be made between them. He cannot
> be their merchant, nor they his customers; and they are all of them thus mutu-
> ally less serviceable to one another. In order to avoid the inconveniency of such
> situations, every prudent man in every period of society, after the first establish-
> ment of the division of labour, must naturally have endeavoured to manage
> his affairs in such a manner, as to have at all times by him, besides the peculiar
> produce of his own industry, a certain quantity of some one commodity or
> other, such as he imagined few people would be likely to refuse in exchange for
> the produce of their industry. (Vol. I, Book I, ch. 4, p. 27)

There are two idioms that have come widely into use explaining the
medium of exchange function, 'nonsynchronization' and 'double coincidence of wants'. A single agent's buying and selling transactions take
place separately − they are nonsynchronous − hence the need for a carrier
of value from the sale to a subsequent purchase. Jevons (1875) explains
why − most purchases are from sellers who do not want what you have
to trade; most sales are to agents from whom you do not want what they
have available; money fills the gap. This is an instance where Shubik's
(1993) term 'strategic decoupler' is particularly apt. Successful barter in
Jevons's terminology requires a 'double coincidence' of wants. But that
is a rare event. More generally, a barter system of decentralized trade
will be overdetermined (impossible generally to implement) if it needs
to fulfill three conditions: budget balance at each pairwise trade; agents
only accepting desired goods and delivering desired sales at each trade;
and eventual complete fulfillment of desired net trades (Starr, 1972). That
overdeterminacy is overcome by freeing up one condition: to arrange for

budget balance in money rather than in real goods. Jevons (1875 [1919], p. 3) describes it this way:

> The earliest form of exchange must have consisted in giving what was not wanted directly for that which was wanted. This simple traffic we call barter . . . and distinguish it from sale and purchase in which one of the articles exchanged is intended to be held only for a short time, until it is parted with in a second act of exchange. The object which thus temporarily intervenes in sale and purchase is money. At first sight it might seem that the use of money only doubles the trouble, by making two exchanges necessary where one was sufficient; but a slight analysis of the difficulties inherent in simple barter shows that the balance of trouble lies quite in the opposite direction. . . . The first difficulty in barter is to find two persons whose disposable possessions mutually suit each other's wants. There may be many people wanting, and many possessing those things wanted; but to allow of an act of barter, there must be a double coincidence, which will rarely happen. . . . Sellers and purchasers can only be made to fit by the use of some commodity . . . which all are willing to receive for a time, so that what is obtained by sale in one case, may be used in purchase in another.

Explicit recognition that the foundations of money as the medium of exchange depend on a 3 × 3 example comes from Wicksell (1898 [1936], p. 21):

> Let us suppose, to take the simplest case, that commodity (A) is desired only by the owners of commodity (B), that commodity (B) is desired by the owners, not of commodity (A), but of a third commodity (C), which, in its turn, is demanded by the possessors of commodity (A) and by no others. It is then obvious that no direct exchange can take place. Only an indirect exchange is possible. For instance, the possessors of (A) might exchange their commodity for commodity (B) with the intention, not of consuming it, but of offering it to the owners of commodity (C), and so of acquiring this commodity (C) which is the one that they desire. But this kind of intermediate trade would soon prove too clumsy and troublesome for any developed economic system unless it were conducted on organised lines. It has therefore become an immemorial custom among all nations to hold stocks of some commodity for which there is a universal demand and to employ it as a *medium of exchange* (in the narrower sense of the term). A commodity is particularly suitable for this purpose if it can be easily transported and if it is not susceptible to rapid decay, so that everyone willingly accepts quantities that are in excess of his immediate requirements. Let us call such a commodity, (M). Then in our example the possessors of commodity (A), assuming that they were provided with a sufficient supply of (M) would obtain the commodity (C), which they desire, in direct exchange for a certain quantity of (M). Then the owners of (C) can use the quantity of (M) which they acquire in this way to buy the commodity (B), and the owners of (B) can then use it to buy the commodity (A). (Original italics)

The 20th-century literature begins to formalize mathematically the notion of transaction costs as Hicks (1935) recommended. First as partial

equilibrium, Baumol (1952), Tobin (1956), Tobin and Golub (1998), and
then in general equilibrium, Foley (1970), Hahn (1971, 1973), Starrett
(1973), Heller (1974), Heller and Starr (1976). This represents the formal
mathematical literature catching up with the 19th-century German language literature. There, it was a commonplace that it was liquidity that
characterized money. Thus Roscher (1878, quoted in Schumpeter, 1954,
p. 1086) comments 'The false definitions of money divide up into two
main groups: those that consider it to be something more, and those that
consider it to be something less, than the most saleable commodity'. The
breakthrough in understanding, unfortunately not followed up by subsequent investigators, comes from Menger (1892). Menger (p. 243) gives us
a working definition of liquidity, *absätzfahigkeit* ('saleability') the spread
between bid and ask prices (or wholesale and retail prices):

> *The theory of money necessarily presupposes a theory of the saleableness
> [Absätzfahigkeit] of goods* [Call] goods . . . more or less saleable, according
> to the . . . facility with which they can be disposed of . . . at current purchas-
> ing prices or with less or more diminution . . . Men . . . exchange goods . . . for
> other goods . . . more saleable [which] become generally acceptable media of
> exchange. (Emphasis in original)

Menger gives us two big ideas here: a functional definition of liquidity
(saleability) and the notion that through repeated use, specialization of the
medium of exchange will become standardized. In Tobin's language, the
designation of a medium of exchange is 'self-justifying' through the liquidity that is a consequence of large-scale usage. This comes about in two
ways: scale economies and learning by doing. If there are scale economies in
transaction costs, then the designation of a common medium of exchange
(be it gold, cattle, or US dollars) creates a natural monopoly; once sufficient
scale in use of the medium of exchange is achieved, it acquires a monopoly
on the medium of exchange function simply because that large scale implies
very low marginal and average transaction costs. Learning by doing is the
same phenomenon dynamically; as traders become increasingly accus-
tomed to a medium of exchange, the transaction costs of using it decline.

## 4    FIAT MONEY

The transition from commodity to paper (or token) money represents a
vast saving in resources for the economy. Money is held as a stock in the
economy. Though it circulates from hand to hand, at any moment there is
a vast stock of money being held. When it is held as relatively unproductive
commodities, such as gold, precious metals, it represents a vast stock of

capital performing useful work, but subject to a major technical improvement. When costly gold can be replaced by virtually costless paper performing the same function, then capital is freed for more productive use.

For a large portion of recorded history, money has meant commodity money, in recent centuries in the form of gold or silver. Paper money consisted of notes backed by a promise to deliver the monetary commodity. We distinguish commodity money and commodity-backed paper money from a currency without commodity backing. An unbacked currency is known as a 'fiat money'.

Money is typically held as an inventory. We hold cash in our wallets; stores hold cash in their tills; households and firms hold balances in checking accounts; banks hold cash in their vaults. Use of a commodity money then implies that the economy will hold large balances of the commodity not for its direct consumption or productive use but rather as the monetary instrument. This inventory of commodity money then constitutes a significant portion of the economy's capital stock, held not for direct production but rather to facilitate the process of trade. A significant resource saving is then possible by substituting paper money for the commodity money. The paper money may consist of banknotes backed by the promise of delivering the monetary commodity on request of the noteholder. This substitution of paper for commodities makes more effective use of the economy's capital. As Adam Smith (1776) notes:

> The substitution of paper in the room of gold and silver money, replaces a very expensive instrument of commerce with one much less costly, and sometimes equally convenient . . . When paper is substituted in the room of gold and silver money, the quantity of . . . capital . . . may be increased by the whole value of gold and silver. . . . The operation . . . resembles that of the undertaker of some great work, who, in consequence of some improvement in mechanics, takes down his old machinery, and adds the difference between its price and that of the new to his . . . capital.
>
> The gold and silver money which circulates in any country . . . is . . . all dead stock. It is a very valuable part of the capital of the country, which produces nothing to the country. The judicious operations of banking, by substituting paper in the room of a great part of this gold and silver, enable the country to convert a great part of this dead stock into active and productive stock. (Vol. I, Book II, ch. 2, p. 350)

Nevertheless, to support a commodity-backed paper currency, a significant quantity of the commodity backing must be maintained in inventory to successfully back the currency.

The next step in economizing on the capital tied up in backing the currency is to use a fiat money. Substituting a government decree for commodity backing frees up a significant fraction of the economy's capital stock for productive use. No longer must the economy hold gold, silver, or other commodities in inventory to back the currency. No longer must additional labor and capital be used to extract them from the earth. Those resources are freed up and a simple virtually costless government decree is substituted for them.

### 4.1  Paradox of Positivity of Value of Fiat Money

Fiat money, an easily recognized portable divisible fiduciary instrument with low transaction and inventory costs, is an ideal medium of exchange if it has positive equilibrium value. But money is what money does. In order to perform the function of a medium of exchange and store of value, money must have a positive value itself (the prices of goods denominated in money terms must be well defined and finite). A government decree that its notes are money does not, however, convey any particular value. Worthless paper printed with the name of the government remains worthless paper. Recalling Lerner's (1947) comment, 'a simple declaration that such and such is money will not do, even if backed by the most convincing constitutional evidence of the state's absolute sovereignty'. Thus, for a fiat money there is always the possibility that it will not be able to serve its function because it may have no value in trade. Equivalently, the price level denominated in fiat money may become infinitely high if participants in the economy are unsure that the currency has a positive value.

### 4.2  Taxation and the Value of Fiat Money

The same government that issues fiat money typically has the power to ensure its value. As Lerner reminds us, simply issuing a decree announcing its value is a meaningless gesture. Prices of goods and conversely the value of currency are determined in the market. But a government with the power to issue currency typically also has the power to tax. It can ensure the value of its currency issue by making it acceptable in payment of taxes due to the state (Starr, 1974; Li and Wright, 1998). The recognition that the power to tax is the power to create a fiat currency goes back to classical economics. Adam Smith (1776) writes, 'A prince, who should enact that a certain proportion of his taxes be paid in a paper money of a certain kind, might thereby give a certain value to this paper money'. (Vol. I, Book II, ch. 2, p. 398)

# 5   A PRICE THEORY OF MONEY

Menger and Hicks, focusing on transaction costs, suggest a research strategy allowing price theory to formulate a theory of the medium of exchange. That theory should be able to provide a foundation for four anomalies in the structure of transactions:

- Trade is monetary. One side of almost all transactions is the economy's common medium of exchange. This observation should be a consequence of low transaction costs in the 'money' and the absence of double coincidence of wants. Chapters 4 and 6 provide examples.
- Money is (locally) unique. Though each economy has a 'money' and the 'money' differs among economies, almost all the transactions in most places most of the time use a single common medium of exchange. This observation should be a consequence of scale economies. In the nature of scale economies, it may be difficult to develop general results, but a large class of examples can easily be presented. Chapter 6 pursues this agenda.
- Money is government-issued fiat money, trading at a positive value though it conveys directly no utility or production. Adam Smith (1776) recognized that government's power to tax implies a positive value to the government fiat money.
- Even transactions displaying a double coincidence of wants are transacted with money. This observation is a surprise. For examples in action, note that University of California faculty whose children are enrolled at the university pay fees in money, not in kind; Ford employees buying a Ford car pay in money, not in kind; Albertson's supermarket checkout clerks acquiring groceries pay in money, not in kind. This observation suggests that the focus on the absence of double coincidence of wants as distinct from transaction costs as an explanation for the monetization of trade may miss a significant part of the underlying causal mechanism. The underlying mechanism here, as noted above, is scale economy or learning by doing. A high-volume exchange (for example, tuition for instruction, or money for groceries) will be the lower-cost arrangement as opposed to barter (lectures for instruction, or labor for groceries).

The balance of this book is designed to formulate a family of general equilibrium models with transaction costs that will develop the four observations above as consequences of the equilibrium, not as assumptions. The bottom line we hope to achieve is that money and monetary institutions are consequences of the market mechanism. Price theory implies monetary theory.

## 5.1 Search and Random Matching

It is useful to distinguish search/random matching models of money (for example, Kiyotaki and Wright, 1989; Trejos and Wright, 1995), from general equilibrium models with transaction cost (for example, Foley, 1970; Hahn, 1971; Starrett, 1973; Ostroy and Starr, 1974; Iwai, 1996; Howitt and Clower, 2000; and this volume). Search models emphasize very imperfect markets with limited ability of traders to locate desirable trades and with limited price flexibility.[2] General equilibrium models typically model complete markets and a fully articulated price system. Using the general equilibrium approach allows us to pursue a parsimonious theory: what is a minimal set of market frictions so that money arises endogenously?

The random matching/search formalization of the friction in trade has a very classical implication: in the rare case where two agents have a double coincidence of wants and meet to trade, they will trade their goods or services directly for one another (Kiyotaki and Wright, 1989; Trejos and Wright, 1995). This is a distinctive feature, distinguishing the random matching/search models from general equilibrium with transaction cost models. In the present model, direct trade between agents with reciprocal demands will take place when that arrangement provides the lowest available transaction cost. This model is further developed in Chapter 5. Hence, even in the rare instance of double coincidence of wants, general equilibrium models with transaction cost need not predict direct trade between parties with reciprocal demands and supplies.

In actual monetary economies, in those comparatively rare instances where double coincidence of wants occurs, it is seldom resolved by barter exchange. Trade between agents – even with a double coincidence of wants – usually takes a monetary form. This is typified by the examples above of a University of California professor's child's university fees, a supermarket checkout clerk's payment for groceries, and an autoworker's purchase of a car. Even in the setting most propitious for barter, those instances where double coincidence of wants occurs, monetary trade prevails. This usage contradicts the predictions of the random matching/search models. It is consistent, however, with Ostroy and Starr (1974, Theorem 4), and it is precisely the behavior that Chapter 6 below would predict.

# 6 SUMMARY FOR THE GENERAL ECONOMIC THEORIST

Most of this volume consists of detailed examples of general equilibrium in economies with a highly segmented transactions structure. Contrary to the Arrow—Debreu model where all goods trade in a single market, where each household faces a single budget constraint, and where each firm has a single expression of profit, the trading post model segments transactions to take place in commodity-pairwise trading markets, with a budget constraint applying to each trader's transaction at each trading post. Most of the underlying logic will be transparent to a practiced general equilibrium theorist. So cutting to the chase, a summary of the results and their basis is presented here.

The treatment in this volume formulates an Arrow—Debreu model with two additional structures: transactions take place at commodity-pairwise trading posts; trade is resource using, requiring transaction costs. Prices at the trading posts are characterized as bid and ask rates of exchange between the goods traded at the post; the bid—ask spread prices transaction costs. At each commodity-pairwise trading post, budget constraints apply separately for each transaction. In an economy of $N$ commodities, there are $\frac{1}{2}N(N-1)$ trading posts, leading to $\frac{1}{2}N(N-1)$ possible budget constraints, reflecting $N(N-1)$ distinct prices. Market equilibrium occurs at prices so that each trading post clears and market makers cover their costs. These complications are sufficient to allow the model to create a market equilibrium with well-defined flows of a medium of exchange. Market segmentation (in trading posts each with its own budget constraint) creates a demand for a carrier of value between trades. Transaction costs create a meaningful choice of which instrument to use as that medium. The most liquid (lowest bid—ask spread) good is the natural money, consistent with Menger's (1892) observations. Segmentation by commodity-pairwise trading posts is a convenient and arbitrary device. The essential point is that it is not simultaneously possible (or economically attractive) to trade all goods together in a single grand trade (as the Arrow—Debreu model posits).

Trading arrangements – autarky, barter, or monetary exchange – are endogenously determined as part of the market equilibrium. A barter equilibrium consists of market-clearing prices so that most of the $\frac{1}{2}N(N-1)$ trading posts are active – goods trade actively against most other goods. A monetary equilibrium, with a commodity money, occurs when most trading posts (though priced) are inactive; the only active posts are those trading the common medium of exchange against all other goods. Liquidity is priced – its price is the bid—ask spread. Commodity money arises endogenously as the most liquid (lowest transaction cost; narrowest bid−ask spread) carrier of value between trading posts. In a model that extends over time, equilibrium money stock and demand for money are well defined.

Following Jevons (1875), it is useful to distinguish the case where there are no complementary arrays of demand and supply (absence of double coincidence of wants versus those with a double coincidence of wants) so that final demands can be satisfied directly by trading unwanted goods for those desired at their common trading post. In an economy with linear transaction costs and absence of double coincidence of wants, where transacton costs differ among goods, it is trivial that the low transaction cost good becomes the common medium of exchange (Chapter 4).

Scale economies in transaction cost, assumed to be large at the level of the trading post, make competitive equilibrium an inappropriate solution concept. The treatment here (Chapter 6) is to use an average cost pricing equilibrium. In this setting, it is difficult to achieve general results characterizing the monetization of equilibrium trading patterns; the treatment here presents a class of examples. Trading posts with scale economies using a medium of exchange create a network externality inducing others' adoption of the same medium. Scale economies in transaction cost account for uniqueness of the (fiat or commodity) money in equilibrium, creating a natural monopoly.

The remaining puzzle is the positive price of fiat (unbacked paper) money. Government-issued fiat money has a positive equilibrium value from its acceptability for tax payments. It sustains the natural monopoly − uniqueness of the fiat money instrument as the medium of exchange − through the scale of government economic activity.

A fully general Arrow−Debreu model without an assumed structure on demand or specialization does not lead to monetary equilibrium with a unique medium of exchange. A fully general treatment includes as a special case Pareto-efficient endowment, resulting in autarky. The general treatment also includes as a special case a demand array of double coincidence of wants and linear transaction costs resulting in a barter equilibrium.

Nevertheless, absent a double coincidence of wants, a linear transaction cost class of examples is sufficient to demonstrate theoretically the first of several practical observations on the monetary character of trade in actual economies:

- Assuming the presence of a low transaction cost instrument, trade is monetary. One side of almost all transactions is the economy's common medium of exchange.

Scale economies in transaction costs create a natural monopoly in the monetary instrument. A class of examples with scale economies demonstrates the commonplace observation that:

- Money is (virtually) unique. Though each economy has a 'money' and the 'money' differs among economies, almost all the transactions in most places most of the time use a single common medium of exchange. Of course the virtually unique money takes many closely related and interchangeable forms: dollar bills, coins, checking accounts, credit card balances, travelers' checks. They are all denominated in the same units and redeemable for one another.

Indeed, scale economies in transaction costs explain an otherwise puzzling empirical observation, that:

- Transactions displaying a double coincidence of wants are transacted with money. University of California faculty enrolling their children in the university pay tuition and fees in money, not in bartered lectures. Supermarket employees buy their groceries for money, not for bartered labor. Trading on the thick markets (money versus tuition; money versus groceries) is a much lower transaction cost undertaking than trading on thin barter markets.

Government's power to tax and fiat money's acceptability in payment of taxes accounts for the positive value of fiat money (Smith, 1776). This observation allows the class of examples, elaborated by the addition of a taxing government, to account for the following:

- Money is government-issued fiat money, trading at a positive value though it conveys directly no utility or production. Further, government's large scale and the underlying scale economies in transaction cost account for the government-issued fiat money becoming the monopoly medium of exchange.

Thus four universal empirical observations above, defining the monetary character of trade, are the result of price theory. This is a success of mathematical economic logic. The foundations of monetary theory do not require significant additional assumptions beyond those of price theory in the context of segmented markets. A logically parsimonious price theoretical model with sufficiently articulated transaction structure is sufficient to develop the monetary structure of trade. The general equilibrium model is particularly well suited to dealing with these issues. Money is necessarily used for trade with many goods and many transactors, hence general equilibrium. The classic Arrow−Debreu model formalizes the common classroom exercise of considering the operation of an economy without money. Then parsimonious sufficient conditions to allow monetization of that model's equilibria constitute weak assumptions sufficient to explain the monetary character of trade in actual economies.

## NOTES

1. Fulfilling the notion of Occam's razor − keeping the model simple and general without unnecessary or restrictive assumptions. This is the mathematician's strategy: keep the assumptions minimal, simple, and general, so that the results can be broadly applicable.
2. Not unlike the approach Smith (1776) presents, quoted above.

# 2.   An economy without money

This chapter introduces the Arrow–Debreu general equilibrium model including futures markets and contingent commodity markets. The result is a model of a successfully functioning economy over time and uncertainty, without money. This model is not a practical proposal, rather it fully represents the classroom exercise of considering how an economy might work without money and monetary institutions. The point of the exercise is to formalize the essential functions of money by demonstrating how the economy would have to adapt in their absence.

## 1   THE ARROW–DEBREU MODEL OF GENERAL EQUILIBRIUM

### 1.1   An Economy without Money

To better understand what money does for us in an economy, a common classroom exercise is to conceive of how an economy would work without money. Economic analysis has actually done quite a thorough job of modeling this idea, known as the Arrow–Debreu model of general equilibrium. Once we understand the complexity of running an economy without money, the comparative ease of a monetary economy becomes evident.

The late James Tobin once explained that the 'inconveniences of barter' consist in how difficult it would be to pay for lodging in a remote town, in a barter economy. Paraphrasing the elaboration in Ostroy and Starr (1974), the explanation goes as follows.

Consider Professor Tobin traveling far from home. He stops at a hotel and asks for lodging for the night. The clerk replies, 'That will be one hundred dollars (unit of account).' Tobin agrees and extracts from the trunk of his car a copy of his latest textbook. 'Here's a copy of my latest textbook. It sells for one hundred dollars (unit of account).' 'Good, here's your room key. Have a pleasant stay.' The hotel keeper trades the book for one hundred dollars' worth of soap. The soap distributor sends the book as payment for detergent, to a detergent manufacturer. The latter pays the book, as dividend, to a stockholder. The stockholder sends the book, as allowance to his son, studying at a major university where Tobin's text is used in a large lecture course. The boy trades the book to a student in the course in exchange for one hundred dollars' worth of contraband, which he consumes.

That is how trade would take place in an ideally coordinated barter economy. The need for coordination arises from the restriction that goods when received must be paid for by a corresponding opposite delivery of goods of equal value, *quid pro quo*. The origins of this restriction are strategic. Without a *quid pro quo* constraint, agents would not be effectively prevented from violating their budget constraints.

The inconveniences of barter consist in the information and coordination implicit in the story at each stage of trade. Only if the hotel keeper knows that his distributor's supplier will accept textbooks in trade is he likely to accept Tobin's book in exchange for lodging. To make a substantial number of transactions depend on trading partners' demands, trading partners' trading partners' demands, trading partners' trading partners' ... trading partners' demands, would make even the simplest trade depend on the communication of massive amounts of data about who trades with whom, when, and what they want. As long as there is a generally acceptable, universally held medium of exchange, no such communication is necessary. Each trade merely consists in the exchange of a desired commodity for the medium of exchange. All one need know about one's trading partners' trading partners is that, like everyone else, they accept the medium of exchange. The informational requirements of 'barter' imply the need for a central coordination of trade; the function of a common medium of exchange is to allow decentralization of the trading process.

## 1.2 The Single Grand Exchange in an Arrow–Debreu Model

The typical household in an Arrow–Debreu model faces one grand budget constraint: income equals outgoings. It sells all of its endowment and receives all of its dividends and then spends all of the proceeds on its consumption plan. There is just one budget constraint: outgoings equals income. In a model over time, consumption includes futures market purchases of dated future consumption and (under uncertainty) contingent commodities. But there is just one budget constraint. There is no separate payment for each of several different purchases. There is no separate income for each of several sources of income. The budget constraint acts as though there were a grand clearinghouse where each household deposits its endowment, is credited book-entry with its value, is similarly credited book-entry with dividend income from its business shares, and then makes purchases limited only by the book-entry value of the budget. It is a post-monetary economy. The typical firm in the Arrow–Debreu economy has a single objective and a single constraint: maximize profits subject to given technology. In a model over time with futures markets, this can be restated as maximize the present discounted value of sales less purchases subject to technology. Here again, there is a single grand transaction: purchase of inputs, delivery of outputs, transmission of dividends, all at once. There are no separate buying and selling transactions. The capital market function, financing current inputs and investment with the value of anticipated future sales, is performed in the futures markets, not through financial transactions. This is true even under uncertainty, where a full set of contingent commodity markets allows the proceeds of sales of future uncertain output to finance current inputs. There can be no role for money in this model. All transactions take place at a single grand complex of trades. There can be no medium of exchange carrying purchasing power between transactions, inasmuch as each transactor makes only one trade. All financial arrangements are undertaken through commodity market mechanisms in a market that meets only once; there can be no store of value.

## 1.3 The Arrow–Debreu Model: A Central Marketplace

The economy consists of firms and households. Each firm has a technology that specifies how it can turn inputs (of labor, capital, intermediate goods) into outputs (of finished goods, services). Each household has an endowment: its own labor, possibly ownership of some land or capital. In addition, households own shares of firms and accept a share of the firms' profits. There is a price-setting mechanism, the Walrasian auctioneer (named after the economist who first fully articulated the general equilibrium model, Léon Walras).

The Walrasian auctioneer calls out prices. The prices are denominated in a numéraire, either one of the existing commodities or a pure number. The units of the prices are unimportant; the important element is relative prices, the ratios (rates of exchange) at which the goods and services can be traded for one another. These ratios tell a household how much labor must be sacrificed for a pound of steak or what the rate of tradeoff is between wine and beer. In response to the prices called out and the implied rates of exchange, firms announce their planned input demands, planned output supplies, and projected profits. Similarly, households recognize their incomes in the value of their endowments and their share of firm profits. The household budget constraint is the restriction that the value of household consumption plans at prevailing prices must be no more than the value of household income (all calculated in the numéraire). Income and prices let the households plan their desired consumptions (consistent with income). Households announce to the auctioneer the supplies (from endowment) they plan to deliver to the market and their demand for goods and services. Based on the announced supply and demand plans of firms and households, the auctioneer calculates excess demands and supplies. Some goods and services may be in surplus at the announced prices, others in shortage.

The Walrasian auctioneer then adjusts the numéraire prices, upward for goods and services in excess demand, downward for those in excess supply. The process is repeated. Firms formulate new plans for inputs to purchase, outputs to produce and sell, and they report new profit levels to their shareholders. Households form new consumption plans based on the new prices and income levels. Firms and households report their buying and selling plans to the Walrasian auctioneer. The auctioneer again computes excess demands and supplies, and once again adjusts prices. This process continues until it converges to market equilibrium, an array of numéraire prices so that demand equals supply for all goods and services. Once the Walrasian auctioneer has found general equilibrium prices (an array of prices for the many goods and services so that supply equals demand for all), he announces the prices to firms and households, and trade proceeds.

How does trade take place in an economy without money? Once equilibrium prices are announced, each firm consults its production technology and chooses a profit-maximizing production plan consisting of a list of inputs to be demanded and outputs to be supplied. It reports its projected profits to shareholders. Households compute the value of endowment and shares of firm profits to determine their available budget. Households plan out desired supplies (from endowment) to the market and desired purchases from the market. Firms and households report their planned supplies and demands to the central clearinghouse. Since prices are general equilibrium prices, supply and demand balance for each good and markets clear.

The mechanics of trade in a nonmonetary setting requires some rethinking. The simplest notion of trade is that there is a central marketplace with a clearinghouse. The firms and households go there and announce their supply and demand plans. The clearinghouse accepts delivery of their supplies and returns their demands to them. Since the prices are equilibrium prices, supply equals demand for each good and there is no unsatisfied demand or undelivered supply (except of free goods).

## 1.4   Futures Contracts

If we accept the nonmonetary trading story above for an economy at a single point in time, there remains the issue of intertemporal allocation.

How do saving and investment decisions take place in an economy without money? A household may have high income at some periods and low income at others. How can it smooth out its consumption? A firm may have highly profitable plans that will pay off in the future. How can it assure needed inputs in the present?

Intertemporal allocation takes place through the use of futures contracts (or dated commodities; Hicks, 1946). Each good and service is described by what it is, and at what date it is to be delivered to the economy. Note that this is common usage in actual commerce for commodities futures contracts (traded, for example, at the Chicago Board of Trade). A commodity (good or service) is defined by what it is, where it is deliverable, and when it is deliverable. Thus, a liter of milk deliverable in Sydney, Australia in 2021 is a different commodity from an otherwise similar liter of milk deliverable in Marseilles in 2023. Both goods will be actively traded and they may have different equilibrium prices.

Thus a firm that needs inputs in 2022 and 2023 to produce saleable output in 2024 buys inputs dated 2022 and 2023 and sells output dated 2024. This is not surprising. The distinctive element of this model is that all of these trades take place on the same market at the same date, prior to any real activity. They are all futures transactions. How does the firm pay for its inputs on the current market, inputs that are deliverable in 2022 and 2023? It pays for them from the value of its sales of output deliverable in 2024. It sells futures contracts on the output and uses the proceeds of the sale to finance the purchase of inputs. Though deliveries of the actual goods and services contracted take place in the future, payment takes place at the market date, prior to production and consumption. Firm profits and household budgets are calculated effective with the market date, far in advance of actual delivery or consumption.

A household with a large endowment to sell in 2021 and 2022 may wish to spread consumption evenly over 2021 to 2045. To do so, the household sells endowment on the currently available futures market and buys consumption deliverable in 2021, 2022, 2023, 2024, . . ., 2045, on the currently available futures markets. The household finances the purchase of consumption in the near to distant future from the proceeds of the sales of futures contracts deliverable in 2021 and 2022.

In this way the futures markets perform the function that in a monetary economy would be performed by the capital markets. Saving and investment are financed through the futures markets rather than in separate capital markets. In equilibrium all of the plans mesh. Firms' projected profits are consistent with projected sales (already contracted) and input requirements (already) contracted. Household consumptions (contracted in advance) are consistent with income from contracted sales of endowment and the household's share of firm profits. Once a full set of market-clearing futures market prices have been determined and contracts bought and sold, the balance of history consists merely in the fulfillment of futures contracts. Markets do not reopen for trade. In the absence of unforeseen events, there is no need or desire to revise plans at prevailing prices.

Firms and households formulate their supply and demand plans (for dated commodities) just as they did above for a single-period economy. The market for their supplies and demands meets before any economic activity (other than the original price adjustment) takes place. The Walrasian auctioneer works just as before, though he has many more commodities and prices to keep track of as have the households and firms. Households and firms report supplies and demands (for dated commodities) to the central clearinghouse and the Walrasian auctioneer adjusts prices so that markets for current goods and for futures contracts clear. The balance of economic activity consists of fulfilling the contracted plans made on the market. At each date households and firms deliver on their promises contracted at the market date and accept delivery of their previously arranged demands. Spot markets do not open at future dates. They have no function. All of the desired supplies and demands have been arranged already on the market for futures contracts.

## 1.5   Uncertainty: Contingent Commodity Contracts

In an economy without money, futures markets are used to overcome the barrier of time. In actual economies financial assets and insurance contracts are also held to overcome uncertainty. How can an economy without money accommodate uncertainty? Though the future is uncertain, it may be possible to write out a list of the possible economically relevant events that can take place in the future. A farmer faces a finite variety of possible future weather conditions. Consumers face a finite variety of unpredictable changes in health and family situation. Firms face a finite variety of shocks to their productivity. Make an exhaustive list of these events. Each one is known as a 'state of the world'.

Now we introduce the notion of a contingent commodity. Households and firms trade in contracts specifying delivery of goods and services at a place, date, and a state of the world. Thus a household may buy an umbrella deliverable next Tuesday in the event that the weather on Tuesday includes rain. A household may buy a medical doctor's attention and a hospital room deliverable in 2015 in the event the household has suffered a major injury then. A household can buy the services of an automobile body shop in 2014 deliverable in the event that the household's car has suffered damage in a collision then.

All of these transactions in an economy without money take place at a single market date prior to the start of economic activity. A household's endowment takes the form of contingent commodities: labor at 2012 (if healthy), labor at 2013 (if healthy), and so forth. A firm's technology shows it how to combine contingent commodities to create contingent output. The prices of these contingent commodities are, however, certain. It's like buying a lottery ticket or an insurance contract. Buyers pay up front whether the uncertain event on which the deal depends occurs or not. The firm computes the value of the inputs it needs and the value of the output it plans. The plans are all contingent on events but the value of inputs and outputs is known at the market date, so the value of firm profits is known at the market date.

The firm reports profits to its shareholders. Households know their income from the sale of contingent commodity endowment (they get paid up front whether delivery is needed or not) and firm profits. Firms and households report their supplies and demands of contingent commodities to the Walrasian auctioneer who adjusts the prices of contingent commodities so that the markets clear. Trade proceeds as before. Firms come to the clearinghouse with a production plan in contingent commodities, acquire their needed (contingent) inputs and sell their planned (contingent) outputs. Households come to the clearinghouse with a portfolio of contingent commodity endowment and leave with a portfolio of contingent commodity planned consumption. The rest of economic activity consists of fulfillment of the firms' and households' contingent plans as events unfold.

## 1.6 What's Wrong with this Picture?

The description above represents how allocation decisions would be implemented in a market economy without money. The processes of price setting, budget constraint enforcement, delivery, and exchange described above are much more centralized and coordinated than in actual economies. Market economists usually seek structures and institutions that are self-enforcing and self-implementing, reflecting the notion of decentralization. The advantages of a monetary economy are implicit in the centralized structure of the economy without money presented above. They show up wherever the representation above differs awkwardly from the everyday usage with which we are familiar.

The first point of greater centralization is in price setting. The Walrasian auctioneer may be a harmless fiction in economic theory, but it reflects a price adjustment process rather more centralized than in actual market economies. Prices in actual economies are set in separate markets: prices for apples and oranges are calculated by those dealing in them independently of the price of cars and steel. In the absence of money, a common medium of exchange and unit of account, those prices must be calculated as buying and selling (ask and bid) rates of exchange between commodity pairs. If there are $N$ goods in the economy, that makes $N(N - 1)$ bid and ask prices. Calculating so many prices, even though only $N$ of them can be independent of one another (by arbitrage − cross-market trading), is an overwhelming task. The price-setting process is far simpler with a common unit of account.

The mechanics of the trading process is too complex in the moneyless economy as well. Though we think of market mechanisms as decentralized, the trading and record-keeping process presented above is centralized in a single clearinghouse. This is not the way trade takes place in actual economies. In actual economies, there are many separate buyers and sellers to deal with, each of whom needs to be sure that those the buyer sells to are not exceeding their budget constraints and that the seller will be compensated when he/she deals with them. A highly centralized accounting system (essentially a checking account system) or a portable currency are effective means of record keeping and enforcing budget constraint. Currency is a fully decentralized means of enforcing budget constraints. The alternative to a common currency is to accept goods in trade, true barter. The difficulty of barter is the complexity of the informational requirements or of the vast number of markets, $\frac{1}{2}N (N - 1)$, that barter requires successfully to implement an economically efficient allocation of resources. The multiplicity of markets or the informational requirements (how do we get goods from those who hold them to those who need them through bilateral, budget-balanced trades?) once again imply great costs or centralization.

The notion of intertemporal trade using futures markets in the moneyless economy above seems farfetched. There are futures markets in actual market economies (for contracts specifying large quantities of agricultural commodities, petroleum, metals, and financial instruments), but their use is over a relatively narrow range of standardized goods. They are not in common usage. Why is that? The transaction costs (broadly conceived) of using futures markets outweigh their benefits. These costs include the out-of-pocket costs of writing and enforcing intertemporal contracts along with the (unpriced) resources used to plan and implement so complex a procedure. These resources include the time and attention of all those active in the markets as well as the cost of procedures to write and implement contracts. It certainly sounds complicated to plan out all of our supply and consumption activities for the indefinite future.

A related reason why full reliance on futures markets for intertemporal allocation is impractical is time discounting. Transaction costs incurred for arranging plans for many years in the future mean incurring costs in the present to implement plans for the future. If there is (explicit or implicit) time discounting of costs, the costs incurred may exceed the (present) value of the benefits from contracting.

The alternative to using a full set of futures markets to plan consumption and production into the future is to use money and debt instruments to move purchasing power over time and to use spot markets to allocate actual goods. Contrary to the futures market economy without money, in this setting markets must reopen over time. A firm requiring inputs in the present to produce profitable output in the future borrows money and buys inputs in the present, sells output and repays debt with money in the future. A household with endowment principally in the present wishing to consume in the future sells endowment and saves (or lends) in the present and uses its savings to purchase consumption in the future. To avoid the costs of futures markets we use spot markets at a sequence of dates and money to carry value between them.

The argument for substituting money and reopening markets for the contingent commodity markets is very similar. It is largely a matter of transaction costs. Having a full set of contingent commodity markets for every good in every contingency in an uncertain world would multiply the number of rather complex markets and the record keeping and enforcement that they require. Since most contingent events will not take place, those transaction costs can be avoided without seriously misallocating resources by recourse to spot markets. Of course, insurance is required to deal with uncertain events, but it can be written in monetary terms (assuming sufficient price foresight on the part of firms and households). Reliance on the vast array of contingent commodity markets with their transaction costs incurred at the market date is prohibitively costly. The economy, and the optimizing agents in it, find that it is far more economical to substitute money, debt, insurance (in money terms), and the reopening of spot markets instead of the elaborate structure of contingent commodities posited in the moneyless economy above.

# 2 EXISTENCE OF GENERAL EQUILIBRIUM IN AN ECONOMY WITH AN EXCESS DEMAND FUNCTION

General equilibrium theory focuses on finding market equilibrium prices for all goods at once. Since there are distinctive interactions across markets (for example, between the prices of oil, gasoline, and the demand for SUVs) it is important that the equilibrium concept include the simultaneous joint determination of equilibrium prices. The concept can then represent a solution concept for the economy as a whole and not merely for a single market that is artificially isolated. General equilibrium for the economy consists of an array of prices for all goods, where simultaneously supply equals demand for each good. The prices of SUVs, oil, and gasoline all adjust so that demand and supply of SUVs, of gasoline, and of oil are each equated.

Let there be a finite number $N$ of goods in the economy. Then a typical array of prices could be represented by an $N$-dimensional vector such as:

$$p = (p_1, p_2, p_3, \ldots, p_{N-1}, p_N) = (3, 1, 5, \ldots, 0.5, 10).$$

The first coordinate represents the price of the first good, the second the price of the second good, and so forth until the $N$th coordinate represents the price of the $N$th good. This expression says that the price of good 1 is three times the price of good 2, that of good 3 is five times the price of good 2, ten times that of good $N - 1$, and half that of good $N$.

We simplify the problem by considering an economy without taking account of money or financial institutions. Only *relative prices* (price ratios) matter here, not monetary prices. This is an assumption common in microeconomic modeling in which the financial structure is ignored. There would be no difference in this model between a situation where the wage rate is $1 per hour and a car costs $1,000 and another where the wage rate is $15 and the same car costs $15,000.

Since only the relative prices matter, and not their numerical values, we can choose to represent the array of prices in whatever numerical values are most convenient. We will do this by confining the price vectors to a particularly convenient set known as the unit simplex. The 'unit simplex' comprises a set of $N$-dimensional vectors fulfilling a simple restriction: Each coordinate of the vectors is nonnegative, and together the $N$ coordinates sum up to 1. We think of a point in the simplex as representing an array of prices for the economy. There is no loss of generality in this formulation. Any possible combination of (nonnegative) relative prices can be represented in this way. To convince yourself of this, simply take any vector of nonnegative prices you wish. Take the sum of the coordinates and divide each term in the vector by this quantity. The result is a vector in the unit simplex reflecting the same relative prices as the original price vector. Hence, without loss of generality we can confine attention to a price space characterized as the unit simplex.

Formally, our price space, the unit simplex in $\mathbf{R}^N$, is:

$$P = \left\{ p \mid p \in \mathbf{R}^N, p_i \geq 0, i = 1, \ldots, N, \sum_{i=1}^{N} p_i = 1 \right\}. \qquad (2.1)$$

The unit simplex is a (generalized) triangle in $N$-space. For $N = 2$, it is a line segment running from $(1, 0)$ to $(0, 1)$; for $N = 3$, it is the triangle with angles (vertices) at $(1,0,0)$, $(0, 1, 0)$, and $(0, 0, 1)$; for $N = 4$, it is a tetrahedron (a three-sided pyramid with triangular sides and base) with vertices at $(1, 0, 0, 0)$, $(0, 1, 0, 0)$, $(0, 0, 1, 0)$, and $(0, 0, 0, 1)$; and so forth in higher dimensions.

A household's demand for consumption or a firm's supply plans are represented as an $N$-dimensional vector. Each of the commodities is represented by a coordinate. We will suppose there is a finite set of households whose names are in the set $H$. For each household $h \in H$, we define a demand function, $D^h(p)$, as a function of the prevailing prices $p \in P$, that is, $D^h : P \rightarrow \mathbf{R}^N$. There is a finite set of firms whose names are in the set $F$, each with a supply function $S^j(p)$, which also takes its values in real $N$-dimensional Euclidean space: $S^j : P \rightarrow \mathbf{R}^N$. Positive coordinates in $S^j(p)$ represent outputs; negative coordinates represent inputs. Hence $p \cdot S^j(p)$ is the value of firm profits (value of outputs minus value of inputs). Each household $h$ has an initial endowment of resources (for example, labor, land, . . .) denoted by the $N$-dimensional vector $r^h$. In addition, household $h$ owns a portion of some firms $j$; the portion is denoted $\alpha^{hj}$, where $0 \leq \alpha^{hj} \leq 1$ and $\Sigma_{h \in H} \alpha^{hj} = 1$. The economy's initial endowment of resources then is $\Sigma_{h \in H} r^h \equiv r \in \mathbf{R}^N$ supplied to the economy. Household $h$'s income consists of the value of endowment it sells and its share of firm profits, so that $h$'s income is $p \cdot r^h + \Sigma_{j \in F} \alpha^{hj} p \cdot S^j(p)$. Household $h$ chooses $D^h(p)$ to optimize utility (or preferences) subject to spending no more than its income.

We combine the individual demand and supply functions to get a market excess demand function representing unfulfilled demands (as positive coordinates) and unneeded supplies (as negative coordinates). The market excess demand function is defined as:

$$Z(p) = \sum_{h \in H} D^h(p) - \sum_{j \in F} S^j(p) - r, \qquad (2.2)$$

$$Z : P \rightarrow \mathbf{R}^N. \qquad (2.3)$$

Each coordinate of the $N$-dimensional vector $p$ represents the price of the good corresponding to the coordinate. The price vector $p$ is $(p_1, p_2, p_3, \ldots, p_N)$, where $p_k$ is the price of good $k$. $Z(p)$ is an $N$-dimensional vector, each coordinate representing the excess demand (or supply if the coordinate has a negative value) of the good represented. $Z(p)$ is

$(Z_1(p), Z_2(p), Z_3(p), \ldots, Z_N(p))$, where $Z_k(p)$ is the excess demand for good $k$. When $Z_k(p)$, the excess demand for good $k$, is negative, we will say that good $k$ is in excess supply. We will assume the following properties on $Z(p)$:

*Walras's Law*:

For all $p \in P$,

$$p \cdot Z(p) = \sum_{i=1}^{N} p_i \cdot Z_i(p) = \sum_{h \in H} p \cdot D^h(p) - \sum_{j \in F} p \cdot S^j(p) - p \cdot r = 0. \quad (2.4)$$

The economic basis for Walras's Law involves the assumption of scarcity and the structure of household budget constraints. $\Sigma_{h \in H} p \cdot D^h(p)$ is the value of aggregate household expenditure. The term $\Sigma_{j \in F} p \cdot S^j(p) + p \cdot r$ is the value of aggregate household income (value of firm profits plus the value of endowment). The Walras's Law says that expenditure equals income.

*Continuity*:

$$Z(p) \text{ is a continuous function.}$$

That is, small changes in $p$ result in small changes in $Z(p)$.

Continuity of $Z(p)$ reflects continuous behavior of household and firm demand and supply as prices change. It includes the economic assumptions of diminishing marginal rate of substitution (*MRS*) for households and diminishing marginal product of inputs for firms.

We assume that $Z(p)$ is well defined and fulfills Walras's Law and Continuity.

The economy is said to be in equilibrium if prices in all markets adjust so that for each good, supply equals demand. When supply equals demand, the excess demand is zero. The exception to this is that some goods may be free and in excess supply in equilibrium. Hence, we characterize equilibrium by the property that for each good $i$, the excess demand for that good is zero (or in the case of free goods, the excess demand may be negative — an excess supply — and the price is zero).

**Definition**    $p^0 \in P$ is said to be an equilibrium price vector if $Z(p^0) \leq 0$ (0 is the zero vector; the inequality applies coordinatewise) with $p_i^0 = 0$ for $i$ such that $Z_i(p^0) < 0$. That is, $p^0$ is an equilibrium price vector if supply equals demand in all markets (with possible excess supply of free goods).

We will now state and prove the major result of this introduction, that under the assumptions introduced above, Walras's Law and Continuity, there is an equilibrium in the economy. To do this we will need one additional piece of mathematical structure, the Brouwer fixed-point theorem:

**Theorem 1** (Brouwer fixed-point theorem) Let $f(\cdot)$ be a continuous function, $f: P \to P$. Then there is $x^* \in P$ so that $f(x^*) = x^*$.

The Brouwer fixed-point theorem is a powerful mathematical result. It takes advantage of the distinctive structure of the simplex. It says that if we have a continuous function that maps points of the simplex back into the simplex (that is, it maps the simplex into itself) then there exists some point on the simplex that is left unchanged in the process. The unchanged point is the fixed point. We can now use this powerful mathematical result to prove a powerful economic result – the existence of general economic equilibrium.

**Theorem 2** (Existence of general economic equilibrium) Let Walras's Law and Continuity be fulfilled. Then there is $p^* \in P$ so that $p^*$ is an equilibrium.

**Proof** The proof of the theorem is the mathematical analysis of an economic story. We suppose prices to be set by an auctioneer. He calls out one price vector $p$, and the market responds with an excess demand vector $Z(p)$. Some goods will be in excess supply at $p$, whereas others will be in excess demand. The auctioneer then does the obvious. He raises the price of the goods in excess demand and reduces the price of the goods in excess supply. But not too much of either change can be made; prices must be kept on the simplex. How should he be sure to keep prices on the simplex? First, the prices have to stay nonnegative. When he reduces a price, he should be sure not to reduce it below zero. When he raises prices, he should be sure that the new resulting price vector stays on the simplex. How? By adjusting the new prices so that they sum up to one. Moreover, we would like to use the Brouwer fixed-point theorem on the price adjustment process; so the auctioneer should make price adjustment a continuous function from the simplex into itself. This leads us to the following price adjustment function $G$, which represents how the auctioneer manages prices.

Let $G: P \to P$, where $G(p) = [G_1(p), G_2(p), \ldots, G_i(p), \ldots, G_N(p),]$. $G_i(p)$ is the adjusted price of good $i$, adjusted by the auctioneer trying to bring supply and demand into balance. The adjustment process of the $i$th price can be represented as $G_i(p)$, defined as follows:

$$G_i(p) \equiv \frac{\max[0, p_i + Z_i(p)]}{\sum_{n=1}^{N} \max[0, p_n + Z_n(p)]}. \tag{2.5}$$

The function $G$ is a price adjustment function. It raises the relative price of goods in excess demand and reduces the price of goods in excess supply while keeping the price vector on the simplex. The expression $p_i + Z_i(p)$ represents the idea that prices of goods in excess demand should be raised and those in excess supply should be reduced. The operator $\max[0, \cdot]$ represents the idea that adjusted prices should be nonnegative. The fractional form of $G$ reminds us that after each price is adjusted individually, they are then readjusted proportionally to stay on the simplex. In order for $G$ to be well defined, we must show that the denominator is nonzero, that is,

$$\sum_{n=1}^{N} \max[0, p_n + Z_n(p)] \neq 0. \tag{2.6}$$

We omit the formal demonstration of (2.6), noting only that it follows from Walras's Law. For the sum in the denominator to be zero or negative, all goods would have to be in excess supply simultaneously, which is contrary to our notions of scarcity and − it turns out − to Walras's Law as well. Recall that $Z(\cdot)$ is a continuous function. The operations of $\max[\ ]$, sum, and division by a nonzero continuous function maintain continuity. Hence, $G(p)$ is a continuous function from the simplex into itself.

By the Brouwer fixed-point theorem there is $p^* \in P$ so that $G(p^*) = p^*$. Because $G(\cdot)$ is the auctioneer's price adjustment function, this means that $p^*$ is a price at which the auctioneer stops adjusting. His price adjustment rule says that once he has found $p^*$ the adjustment process stops.

Now we have to show that the auctioneer's decision to stop adjusting the price is really the right thing to do. That is, we would like to show that $p^*$ is not just the stopping point of the price adjustment process, but that it actually does represent general equilibrium prices for the economy. We therefore must show that at $p^*$, all markets clear with the possible exception of a few with free goods in oversupply.

Since $G(p^*) = p^*$, for each good $k$, $G_k(p^*) = p_k^*$. That is, for all $k = 1, \ldots, N$,

$$p_k^* = \frac{\max[0, p_k^* + Z_k(p^*)]}{\sum_{n=1}^{N} \max[0, p_n^* + Z_n(p^*)]}. \tag{2.7}$$

Looking at the numerator in this expression, we can see that the equation will be fulfilled either by:

$$p_k^* = 0 \quad \text{(Case 1)} \tag{2.8}$$

or by

$$p_k^* = \frac{p_k^* + Z_k(p^*)}{\sum_{n=1}^{N} \max[0, p_n^* + Z_n(p^*)]} > 0 \quad \text{(Case 2).} \tag{2.9}$$

Case 1: $p_k^* = 0 = \max[0, p_k^* + Z_k(p^*)]$. Hence, $0 \geq p_k^* + Z_k(p^*) = Z_k(p^*)$ and $Z_k(p^*) \leq 0$. This is the case of free goods with market clearing or with excess supply in equilibrium.

Case 2: To avoid repeated messy notation, let

$$\lambda = \frac{1}{\sum_{n=1}^{N} \max[0, p_n^* + Z_n(p^*)]} \tag{2.10}$$

so that $G_k(p^*) = \lambda[p_k^* + Z_k(p^*)]$. Since $p^*$ is the fixed point of $G$ we have $p_k^* = \lambda[p_k^* + Z_k(p^*)] > 0$. This expression is true for all $k$ with $p_k^* > 0$, and $\lambda$ is the same for all $k$. Let us perform some algebra on this expression. We first combine terms in $p_k^*$:

$$(1 - \lambda)p_k^* = \lambda Z_k(p^*), \tag{2.11}$$

then multiply through by $Z_k(p^*)$ to get:

$$(1 - \lambda)p_k^* Z_k(p^*) = \lambda[Z_k(p^*)]^2, \tag{2.12}$$

and now sum over all $k$ in Case 2, obtaining:

$$(1 - \lambda) \sum_{k \in \text{Case2}} p_k^* Z_k(p^*) = \lambda \sum_{k \in \text{Case2}} [Z_k(p^*)]^2. \tag{2.13}$$

Walras's Law says:

$$0 = \sum_{k=1}^{N} p_k^* Z_k(p^*) = \sum_{k \in \text{Case1}} p_k^* Z_k(p^*) + \sum_{k \in \text{Case2}} p_k^* Z_k(p^*). \tag{2.14}$$

But for $k \in$ Case 1, $p_k^* Z_k(p^*) = 0$, and so:

$$0 = \sum_{k \in \text{Case1}} p_k^* Z_k(p^*). \tag{2.15}$$

Therefore,

$$\sum_{k \in \text{Case2}} p_k^* Z_k(p^*) = 0. \tag{2.16}$$

Hence, we have

$$0 = (1 - \lambda) \cdot \sum_{k \in \text{Case2}} p_k^* Z_k(p^*) = \lambda \cdot \sum_{k \in \text{Case2}} [Z_k(p^*)]^2. \tag{2.17}$$

Using Walras's Law, we established that the left-hand side equals 0, but the right-hand side can be zero only if $Z_k(p^*) = 0$ for all $k$ such that $p_k^* > 0$ ($k$ in Case 2). Thus, $p^*$ is an equilibrium. This concludes the proof. QED

The demonstration here is striking; it displays the essential economic and mathematical elements of the proof of the existence of general equilibrium. These are the use of a fixed-point theorem, of Walras's Law, and of the continuity of excess demand. If the economy fulfills continuity and Walras's Law, then we expect it to have a general equilibrium. The mathematics that assures us of this result is a fixed-point theorem.

## 3   ALLOCATIVE EFFICIENCY OF THE GENERAL EQUILIBRIUM

The existence of general equilibrium prices is only half of the good news here. It is a remarkable result in itself: a decentralized uncoordinated process among many households and firms, mediated only by a price system, with a responsive price adjustment process, can achieve an internally consistent result.

But there's more! Not only is the result internally consistent (market clearing). It is also desirable! More precisely, the resulting allocation of resources is Pareto efficient. The Pareto efficiency property says that all of the opportunities for reallocating resources to more productive uses have been fully utilized. It says that all of the opportunities for reallocating consumption among households for mutually more satisfactory consumption plans have been fully utilized.

Stated more formally,

**Theorem 3** (First fundamental theorem of welfare economics) Let $p \in P; y^j = S^j(p)$, all $j \in F; x^h = D^h(p)$, all $h \in H$ be a competitive equilibrium price and allocation array of the Arrow−Debreu model economy. Then the production allocation $y^j, j \in F$ and the consumption allocation $x^h, h \in H$ constitutes a Pareto-efficient (Pareto-optimal) allocation.

Just as Adam Smith (1776) relied on an invisible hand, so modern general equilibrium theorists rely on the first fundamental theorem of welfare economics to explain the effectiveness (not necessarily fairness) of a market allocation. As we investigate the workings of a monetary economy in subsequent chapters, this optimistic result undergoes some unhappy transformation. Though a small subclass of monetary equilibria remains Pareto efficient, the transaction costs and multiplicity of budget balancing requirements that monetization is intended to overcome necessarily reduce allocative efficiency. These topics are developed in Chapter 12.

# 3.  The trading post model[1]

The trading post model consists of $N$ commodities traded pairwise at $\frac{1}{2}N(N-1)$ trading posts with distinct bid and ask prices reflecting transaction costs. Households create trading plans to optimize utility subject to prevailing prices and subject to a budget constraint at each post. A barter equilibrium will occur if most trading posts are active in equilibrium – most goods trading directly for most other goods. A monetary equilibrium occurs if active trade is concentrated on a few trading posts, those trading the common medium of exchange against most other goods.

In Chapter 2 we examined the moneyless Arrow–Debreu model. It did not use money since all transactions were with a central market in a single instance, with a single budget constraint. There could be no role for a carrier of value between transactions when each agent or firm made *only one* transaction, however large. It is well known that a frictionless Arrow–Debreu model cannot accommodate a role for money. The single budget constraint facing transactors in the model precludes a carrier of value between transactions. The key to bringing money into the model is to let there be many transactions, each of which requires a payment for purchases or receives payment for sales. This can be achieved by reopening trade over time (Hahn, 1971, 1973; Starrett, 1973; Wallace, 1980), by randomly bringing households into contact for limited trading opportunities (Kiyotaki and Wright, 1989), or by segmenting the trading opportunities. The last approach will be pursued here.

The underlying concept is that the model should follow Hicks's suggestion: 'look the frictions in the face'. In the overlapping generations model, the friction is the difficulty of trading goods over time when there is no match in commodities sellers have and buyers demand. In the random matching model the friction is the absence of double coincidence of wants combined with the difficulty in repayment when buyer and seller need never meet again.

The trading post model decomposes the trading plans of each household into many separate transactions. An earlier generation of monetary economists would have called this 'non-synchronization'. Buying and selling transactions, though they equal each other in value so that budgets balance, take place at separate transactions. Hence a carrier of value is required between them. Formalization of this notion takes the following form. There are $N$ commodities in the economy. Then there are $\frac{1}{2}N(N-1)$ commodity pairs, and for each there is a trading post where the two goods are traded for each other. A budget constraint applies at each trading post – you pay for what you get at each transaction separately. Like all models, this is not completely realistic. It is designed to substitute many payment obligations for the single grand budget constraint of the Arrow–Debreu model. It emphasizes the multiplicity of budget constraints and the need for means of payment to carry value from one to another.

The pattern of active trade is endogenously determined as part of the equilibrium of the trading post economy. A barter equilibrium will occur if most trading posts are active, most goods trading directly for most other goods. In a monetary equilibrium, most trading posts will be inactive. A single or small number of goods will be determined as (commodity) 'money'. Trading posts dealing in 'money' for most other goods will be active in a monetary equilibrium. The pattern of endowments and demands, the dynamics of the price mechanism and transaction costs will determine the equilibrium array of trading post activity.

Most models of money as a medium of exchange, following Jevons (1875) (see Ostroy and Starr, 1974, Kiyotaki and Wright, 1989, and the models discussed in Ostroy and Starr, 1990) focus on trade as an interaction between individual agents in the economy – the primitive unit is the pair of traders. The present study, following Walras's discussion below, treats the primitive unit as pairs of commodities in which active trade takes place. In this it follows the approach of Rogawski and Shubik (1986), and of Shubik (1973, 1993). Shapley and Shubik (1977) and Starr (2003a,b) also treat the trading post model (see also Banerjee and Maskin, 1996 and Howitt, 2005).

Walras (1874 [1954], p. 158) forms the picture this way (assuming $m$ distinct commodities):

> we shall imagine that the place which serves as a market for the exchange of all the commodities (A), (B), (C), (D) . . . for one another is divided into as many sectors as there are pairs of commodities exchanged. We should then have $\frac{m(m-1)}{2}$ special markets each identified by a signboard indicating the names of the two commodities exchanged there as well as their . . . rates of exchange . . .

Following Walras, the treatment in this book will conceive of the market for $N$ commodities as composed of $\frac{1}{2}N(N-1)$ commodity-pairwise trading posts. The distinctive modeling approach – what makes this a monetary model – is that in addition, we suppose that there is a budget balance condition at each post. Each good acquired at the post must be paid for by an equivalent delivery of the other good traded there.

It is this multiplicity of budget constraints that creates the demand for a carrier of value between trading posts. Whereas one post may be attractive for sales of endowment or other supplies, another may be more suitable for desired purchases. A carrier of value between trading posts is then required to allow sales at one post to fund purchases at the next. The typical worker sells labor − not directly for desired consumption, but rather for a medium of exchange − and then acquires desired consumption not in direct exchange for labor but rather in trade for the medium of exchange. This arrangement will be shown to be a general equilibrium outcome of the trading post model with its corresponding multiplicity of budget constraints.

Starting from the nonmonetary Arrow−Debreu model, two additional structures are sufficient to give endogenous monetization in equilibrium: multiple budget constraints (one at each transaction, not just on net trade) and transaction costs. The choice of which trading posts a typical household will trade at is part of the household optimization. The equilibrium structure of exchange is the array of trading posts that actually host active trade. The determination of which trading posts are active in equilibrium is endogenous to the model and characterizes the monetary character of trade. The equilibrium is monetary with a unique money if only $(N - 1)$ trading posts are active, those trading all goods against 'money'.

Let there be $N$ commodities, numbered $1, 2, \ldots, N$. Goods are traded in pairs − good $i$ for good $j$ − at specialized trading posts. The trading post for trade of good $i$ versus good $j$ (and vice versa) is designated $\{i, j\}$; trading post $\{i, j\}$ is the same trading post as $\{j, i\}$. Trading post $\{i, j\}$ is a business firm, the market maker in trade between goods $i$ and $j$. $\{i, j\}$ actively buys and (re)sells both $i$ and $j$. Trade as a resource-using activity is modeled by describing the post's transaction costs. The notion of transaction cost summarizes costs that in an actual economy are incurred by retailers, wholesalers, individual firms and households. The bid−ask spread summarizes these costs to the model's transactors. Thus, part of transaction cost represents the (nonmarketed) time and resources used by households in arranging their transactions, summarized here imprecisely as a price spread.[2]

The spread between bid (price at which the public can sell) and ask (price at which the public can buy) prices is explicit in financial markets. The difference between them is the return to the market maker for maintaining an active market. More colloquially we might think of it as the difference between wholesale (bid) and retail (ask) prices. This usage was introduced to general equilibrium models with transaction costs by Foley (1970) and Hahn (1971). The combination of a multiplicity of budget constraints and transaction costs made explicit in the spread between bid and ask prices allows a clear specification of the friction needed to make money useful.

Specify a transaction cost function for these pairwise trading posts. An awkward but parsimonious convention is then that transaction costs incurred are defrayed through the surplus of goods $i$ and $j$ left with the trading post on completion of trade. This (iceberg model) is obviously a restrictive convention, but it simplifies accounting for transaction costs. The typical transactions of trading post $\{i, j\}$ will consist of purchases $y_i^{\{i,j\}B}, y_j^{\{i,j\}B} \geq 0$ of $i, j$, and sales $y_i^{\{i,j\}S}, y_j^{\{i,j\}S} \geq 0$ of $i$ and $j$.

A linear transaction cost function[3] for trading post $\{i, j\}$ is:

$$C^{\{i,j\}} = \delta^i y_i^{\{i,j\}B} + \delta^j y_j^{\{i,j\}B} \quad \text{(TCL)}$$

where $\delta^i, \delta^j > 0$. In words, the transaction technology looks like this: trading post $\{i, j\}$ makes a market in goods $i$ and $j$, buying each good in order to resell it. Transaction costs vary directly (in proportions $\delta^i, \delta^j$) with volume of trade. The transaction cost structure is separable in the two principal traded goods.

The nonconvex (scale economy) cost function[4] for trading post $\{i, j\}$ is:

$$C^{\{i,j\}} = \min[\delta^i y_i^{\{i,j\}B}, \gamma^i] + \min[\delta^j y_j^{\{i,j\}B}, \gamma^j], \quad \text{(TCNC)}$$

where $\delta^i, \delta^j, \gamma^i, \gamma^j > 0$. In words, the transaction technology looks like this: trading post $\{i, j\}$ makes a market in goods $i$ and $j$, buying each good in order to resell it. Transaction costs vary directly (in proportions $\delta^i, \delta^j$) with volume of trade at low volume and then hit a ceiling after which they do not increase with trading volume. The specification in (TCNC) is an extreme case: zero marginal transaction cost beyond the ceiling. Adding additional linear terms would represent a more general case.

The trading post $\{i, j\}$ defrays the transaction cost $C^{\{i,j\}}$ through the retained $i$ and $j$ left with the post through the difference between the bid and ask prices, covering the transaction costs it incurs in goods $i$ and $j$. The transaction cost function $C^{\{i,j\}}$ is sufficiently flexible to distinguish transaction costs differing among commodities, including differences in durability, portability, recognizability, divisibility. However, the transaction cost structure posited here is surely oversimplified: transaction costs are assessed only in the goods transacted. This simplifies the accounting for cost. The usage ignores that transaction costs are incurred in labor, capital, additional resources.

This volume – with the exception of the transaction technologies (and of some generalization with no increase in complexity in Chapter 12) – will deal with a pure exchange economy. Since the focus of the study is the role of transactions, budgets, and transaction cost, that simplification seems appropriate.

The population of households is denoted $H$, consisting of a mix of subpopulations (with different tastes and endowments). Jevons reminds us that the mix of household tastes is essential to the discussion of media of exchange. For example, if the endowment allocation is Pareto efficient, then there will be no exchange in equilibrium and no medium of exchange. Conversely, Jevons insists that if the endowment allocation displays absence of double coincidence of wants, then indirect trade and use of a medium of exchange is likely to result. Alternatively, Jevons suggests (more on this later) that if the endowment allocation displays double coincidence of wants then direct trade is likely to result in equilibrium, with no common medium of exchange.

Specifying the tastes and endowment then is an essential step. We shall do that separately in each chapter, emphasizing the role of absence of double coincidence of wants in some, its presence in others.

A typical household $h \in H$, has an endowment $r^h \in \mathbf{R}^N_+$; $r^h_n$ is $h$'s endowment of good $n$.

Households formulate their trading plans deciding how much of each good to trade at each pairwise trading post. This is very much the calculation they performed in the Arrow−Debreu model of Chapter 2, but the trading post context makes for more detail. This leads to the rather messy notation:

$b^{h\{i,j\}}_\ell$ = planned purchase of good $\ell$ by household $h$ at trading post $\{i,j\}$.

$s^{h\{i,j\}}_\ell$ = planned sale of good $\ell$ by household $h$, at trading post $\{i,j\}$.

There is some redundant generality in this notation, since the only goods actually traded at $\{i,j\}$ will be $i$ and $j$.

The bid prices (the prices at which the trading post will buy from households) at $\{i,j\}$ are $q^{\{i,j\}}_i$, $q^{\{i,j\}}_j$ for goods $i$ and $j$, respectively. The price of $i$ is in units of $j$. The price of $j$ is in units of $i$. The ask price (the price at which the trading post will sell to households) of $j$ is the inverse of the bid price of $i$ (and vice versa). That is, $(q^{\{i,j\}}_i)^{-1}$ and $(q^{\{i,j\}}_j)^{-1}$ are the ask prices of $j$ and $i$ at $\{i,j\}$. The trading post $\{i,j\}$ covers its costs by the difference between the bid and ask prices of $i$ and $j$, that is, by the spread $(q^{\{i,j\}}_j)^{-1} - q^{\{i,j\}}_i$ and the spread $(q^{\{i,j\}}_i)^{-1} - q^{\{i,j\}}_j$. Transaction costs at the trading post are incurred in goods $i$ and $j$, acquired in trade through the difference in bid and ask prices.

Given $q^{\{i,j\}}_i$, $q^{\{i,j\}}_j$, for all $\{i,j\}$, household $h$ then forms its buying and selling plans, in particular deciding which trading posts to use to execute its desired trades. Household $h \in H$ faces the following constraints on its transaction plans. Since these recur in subsequent chapters they probably deserve a name, 'Trading post balance constraints':

(T.i) $b_n^{h\{i,j\}} > 0$ only if $n = i, j$; $s_n^{h\{i,j\}} > 0$ only if $n = i, j$.

(T.ii) $b_i^{h\{i,j\}} \le q_j^{\{i,j\}} \cdot s_j^{\{i,j\}}$, $b_j^{h\{i,j\}} \le q_i^{\{i,j\}} \cdot s_i^{\{i,j\}}$ for each $\{i,j\}$.

(T.iii) $x_n^h = r_n^h + \Sigma_{\{i,j\}} b_n^{h\{i,j\}} - \Sigma_{\{i,j\}} s_n^{h\{i,j\}} \ge 0, 0 \le n \le N$.

Note that condition (T.ii) defines a budget balance requirement at the transaction level, implying the decentralized character of trade. Since the budget constraint applies to each pairwise transaction separately, there may be a demand for a carrier of value to move purchasing power between distinct transactions. $h$ faces the array of bid prices $q_i^{\{i,j\}}$, $q_j^{\{i,j\}}$ and chooses $s_n^{h\{i,j\}}$ and $b_n^{h\{i,j\}}$, $n = i, j, i, j = 1, 2, \ldots, N, i \ne j$, to maximize $u^h(x^h)$ subject to (T.i), (T.ii), (T.iii). That is, $h$ chooses which pairwise markets to transact in and a transaction plan to optimize utility, subject to a multiplicity of pairwise budget constraints.

In the case of a linear transaction technology, characterized by (TCL), a competitive equilibrium is an appropriate solution concept resulting in zero profits for the typical trading post (with the additional benefit that no account need be taken of distribution of profits). The threat of entry (by other similar trading post firms) rationalizes the competitive model, but for simplicity we take there to be a unique trading post firm making a market in goods $i$ and $j$, denoted indiscriminately $\{i, j\} = \{j, i\}$.

Market equilibrium will be described similarly for the linear (TCL) and scale economy (TCNC) cases. Both require a zero profit condition for the trading posts. The zero-profit condition is an elementary outcome of competition in the linear model. In the scale economy setting, it is a useful simplification. Both require price-taking optimization for households. Thus, in the description below, the household will choose a trading plan among trading posts that optimizes utility subject to the trading post balance constraints at prevailing prices. This is completely consistent with the price-taking optimization posited in Chapter 2's Arrow–Debreu model, recast in the much more detailed setting of the trading post model with bid and ask prices. That is the significance of the first bulleted quality. Market clearing at each trading post is the second.

A *market equilibrium* consists of $q_i^{o\{i,j\}}$, $q_j^{o\{i,j\}}$, $1 \le i, j \le N$, so that:

- For each household $h \in H$, there is a utility-optimizing plan $b_n^{oh\{i,j\}}$, $s_n^{oh\{i,j\}}$ (subject to T.i, T.ii, T.iii) so that $\Sigma_h b_n^{oh\{i,j\}} = y_n^{o\{i,j\}S}$, $\Sigma_h s_n^{oh\{i,j\}} = y_n^{o\{i,j\}B}$, $n = i, j$, for each $\{i,j\}$, each $n$, where:
- $y_n^{o\{i,j\}S} \le y_n^{o\{i,j\}B}$, $n = i, j$.
- $y_i^{o\{i,j\}B} - y_i^{o\{i,j\}S} + y_j^{o\{i,j\}B} - y_j^{o\{i,j\}S} = C^{\{i,j\}}$ for all $1 \le i, j \le N, i \ne j$.

The expression in the last bullet is a zero profit condition.

An equilibrium is said to be **'monetary'** with a unique money, $\mu$, if — for all households — good $\mu$ is the only good that a household will both buy and sell. An equilibrium will be monetary with multiple moneys, $\mu^1, \mu^2, \ldots$, if — for all households — $\mu^1, \mu^2, \ldots$ are the only goods that a household will both buy and sell.

## NOTES

1. This chapter is based on the model in Starr (2003, 2004).
2. In Chapter 10, we let households deal with their transaction costs internally and avoid characterizing them as a bid−ask spread. An alternative more explicit treatment of household nonmarket transaction cost decisions is embodied in Kurz (1974).
3. (TCL) is intended as a mnemonic for linear transaction cost.
4. (TCNC) is intended as a mnemonic for nonconvex transaction cost.

# 4.   An elementary linear example: liquidity creates money[1]

This chapter considers a pure exchange trading post economy with linear transaction costs. One commodity has, by assumption, distinctively low transaction cost. Bid and ask prices for all goods in exchange for the low transaction cost good reflect its low transaction cost, creating a narrow bid–ask spread. In general equilibrium and assuming the absence of double coincidence of wants, the low transaction cost commodity becomes the common medium of exchange. Its specialization as the common medium of exchange is the result of decentralized exchange and competitive pricing. There is no role for government, legal tender, or consensus. Monetization is fully decentralized.

## 1   THE MOST SALEABLE GOOD

The most elementary function of money – the medium of exchange – is as a carrier of value held between successive transactions. Carl Menger (1892 p. 243) reminds us that the distinguishing feature of the medium of exchange should be liquidity:

> [W]hy . . . is . . . economic man . . . ready to accept a certain kind of commodity, *even if he does not need it* . . . in exchange for all the goods he has brought to market[?] . . . *The theory of money necessarily presupposes a theory of the saleableness [Absätzfahigkeit] of goods* [Call] goods . . . *more or less saleable*, according to the . . . facility with which they can be disposed of . . . at current purchasing prices or with less or more diminution . . . Men . . . exchange goods . . . for other goods . . . more saleable [which] become generally acceptable media of exchange. (Emphasis in original) [2]

'Saleableness' is liquidity. Though Menger notes many dimensions to liquidity (delay, uncertainty, search, . . .), a simple characterization is the difference between the bid price and the ask price. A commodity that acts as a medium of exchange is necessarily repeatedly bought (accepted in trade) and sold (delivered in trade). Therefore a good with a narrow spread between bid and ask price is priced to encourage households to use it as a carrier of value between trades, as a medium of exchange with relatively low cost.

Consistent with the approach of this volume, we posit a trading post model. The pattern of trade across trading posts is determined endogenously. A 'barter' equilibrium occurs when most trading posts are active in equilibrium, one for each pair of distinct goods. Conversely, if most trading posts are inactive in equilibrium, and there is active trade concentrating on the small number of posts trading a single good pairwise against all others, then the equilibrium will be described as *'monetary'*, with the single commonly traded good as 'commodity money'.

## 2   HOUSEHOLDS

Consider a pure exchange trading post economy with $N$ commodities, $N \geq 3$. $\Omega$ denotes the greatest integer $\leq (N - 1)/2$.

Let $[i, j]$ denote a household endowed with good $i$ that prefers good $j$; $i \neq j, i, j = 1, 2, \ldots, N$. Household $[i, j]$'s endowment is 1 unit of commodity $i$. Denote the endowment of $[i, j]$ as $r_i^{[i,j]} = 1$. $[i, j]$'s utility function is $u^{[i,j]}(x_1, x_2, x_3, \ldots, x_N) = x_j$. That is, household $[i, j]$ values good $j$ only. It cares for $i$ only as a resource to trade for $j$. This is obviously an immense oversimplification − but it serves to focus the issue.

Consider a population denoted $\Theta$ of households displaying a complete absence of double coincidence of wants. There are $\Omega$ households endowed with each good and each household desires a good different from its endowment. There are $\Omega$ households endowed with good 1, preferring respectively, goods 2, 3, 4, . . ., $\Omega + 1$: [1, 2], [1, 3], [1, 4], . . ., [1, $\Omega + 1$]. There are $\Omega$ households endowed with good 2, preferring respectively goods 3, 4, 5, . . ., $\Omega + 2$: [2, 3], [2, 4], [2, 5], . . ., [2, $\Omega + 2$]. The roll call of households proceeds through [$N$, 1], [$N$, 2], [$N$, 3], . . ., [$N$, $\Omega$].

One way to think of $\Theta$ is that its elements $[i,j]$ are set round a clock-face at a position corresponding to the endowed good, $i$, eager to acquire $j$, $j$ being 1, 2, . . ., $\Omega$, steps clockwise from $i$. Population $\Theta$ displays absence of the 'double coincidence of wants' that Jevons (1875) posits allows successful barter. That is the rare event where traders can directly, without an intermediary good, arrange pairwise mutually improving trades. An exchange of good $i$ for good $j$ then includes one trader with an excess supply of $i$ and an excess demand for $j$, and a second trader with the opposite unsatisfied supply and demand. In this example, on the contrary, for each household endowed with good $i$ and desiring good $j$, $[i,j]$, there is no precise mirror image, $[j, i]$. Nevertheless, there are $\Omega$ households endowed with one unit of commodity 1, and $\Omega$ households strongly preferring commodity 1 to all others. That is true for each good. Thus gross supplies equal gross demands, though there is no immediate opportunity for any two households to make a mutually advantageous trade. Jevons tells us that this is precisely the setting where money is suitable to facilitate trade.

## 3 *QUID PRO QUO*

Recall the trading post balance constraints, T.i, T.ii, T.iii. Budgets must balance at each trading post − that is, you pay for what you get not only over the course of all trade (as in the Arrow−Debreu model) but at each trading post separately. A household delivers good $i$ to trading post $\{i, j\}$ and the delivery is evaluated at the post's bid price determining how much good $j$ the household receives. Budget balance requires that the values be equal.

## 4 TRANSACTION COSTS AND PRICES

Consider trading posts with a linear transaction cost structure. The trading post buys goods from households and resells them or retains them to cover transaction costs. Let the cost structure of trading post $\{i, j\}$, $i, j = 1, 2, \ldots, N, i \neq j, i \neq m \neq j$, be:

$$C^{\{i,j\}} = \delta \times \text{(volume of goods } i \text{ and } j \text{ purchased by the post) (TCL)}$$

Marginal cost of trading $i$ for $j$ is $\delta$ times the gross quantity traded. The trading post expects to cover its transaction costs through the bid−ask spread.

Trading good $m$ is assumed to be costless. This is where the fix goes in − $m$ is being set up as the natural money. We shall see how that works out in equilibrium. Thus,

$$C^{\{m,j\}} = \delta \times \text{(volume of good } j \text{ purchased by the post) (TCL),}$$

for $j = 1, 2, \ldots, m - 1, m + 1, \ldots, N$.

Trading post $\{1, 2\}$ accepts good 1 in exchange for good 2 and accepts good 2 in exchange for good 1. Prices are expressed as a rate of exchange between goods 1 and 2. That is, good 1 is priced in units of good 2 and good 2 is priced in units of good 1. In order to cover the post's operating costs, the prices at which the public buys (ask or retail prices) are higher than those at which the public sells (bid or wholesale prices). The difference between buying and selling prices covers operating costs.

Restating the trading post model of Chapter 3. At trading post $\{i, j\}$, the ask price of $j$ (denominated in $i$ per unit $j$) is the inverse of the bid price of $i$ (denominated in $j$ per unit $i$). Denote the bid price of good $i$ at $\{i, j\}$ as $q_i^{\{i,j\}}$. Then the ask price of $j$ is $[q_i^{\{i,j\}}]^{-1}$. Denote the purchase of $i$ by a typical household $h$ at $\{i, j\}$ as $b_i^{h\{i,j\}}$, sale of $j$ as $s_j^{h\{i,j\}}$. Then the budget constraint facing household $h$ at $\{i, j\}$ is $b_i^{h\{i,j\}} = s_j^{h\{i,j\}} q_j^{\{i,j\}}$. Household $h$'s consumption of good $i$ then is $x_i^h \equiv r_i^h + \sum_{j=1}^N [b_i^{h\{i,j\}} - s_i^{h\{i,j\}}]$.

In an economy of $N$ commodities there are $\frac{1}{2}N(N-1)$ trading posts each with two posted prices (bid price for one good in terms of a second, and bid price of the second in units of the first) totaling $N(N-1)$ pairwise price ratios. Prices are posted at all trading posts — including those without active trade.

The market equilibrium guided by the price system here must answer the question: which trading posts operate at positive trading volume? In actual economies, most conceivable pairwise commodity trades do not occur. A trading post becomes unattractive in equilibrium, and will have zero trading volume (a corner solution), when its bid–ask spread is wide enough to discourage trade.

# 5   MARGINAL COST PRICING EQUILIBRIUM

Restating the market-clearing equilibrium concept of Chapter 3, an array of prices $q_i^{o\{i,j\}}$ and trades $b_i^{oh\{i,j\}}$, $s_j^{oh\{i,j\}}$ for $h \in \Theta$ is said to be a *marginal cost pricing equilibrium* if each household $h \in \Theta$ optimizes utility subject to budget at prevailing prices, each trading post clears, and trading posts cover marginal costs through bid–ask spreads.

More formally, a marginal cost pricing equilibrium under the transaction cost function above consists of $q_i^{o\{i,j\}}$, $q_j^{o\{i,j\}}$, $1 \le i, j \le N$, $i \ne j$, so that:

- For each household $h \in \Theta$, there is a utility-optimizing plan $b_n^{oh\{i,j\}}$, $s_n^{oh\{i,j\}}$ so that:

$$b_i^{oh\{i,j\}} = s_j^{oh\{i,j\}} q_j^{o\{i,j\}} \text{ (budget balance).}$$

- For each $i, j, i \ne j$,

$$\sum_h b_n^{oh\{i,j\}} \le \sum_h s_n^{oh\{i,j\}}, n = i, j \text{ (market clearing);}$$

- For $i = 1, \ldots, N; j = 1, 2, \ldots, N; i \ne j; i, j \ne m$,

$$\delta \times \Sigma_{h\in\Theta}[s_i^{oh\{i,j\}} + s_j^{oh\{i,j\}}] = \Sigma_{h\in\Theta}([s_i^{oh\{i,j\}} - b_i^{oh\{i,j\}}] + [s_j^{oh\{i,j\}} - b_j^{oh\{i,j\}}]).$$

- For $i = 1, \ldots, N; i \neq m,$

$$\delta \times \Sigma_{h\in\Theta}[s_i^{oh\{i,m\}}] = \Sigma_{h\in\Theta}([s_i^{oh\{i,m\}} + b_i^{oh\{i,m\}}] - [s_m^{oh\{i,m\}} - b_m^{oh\{i,m\}}])$$

(transaction cost coverage).

The concluding expressions are (linear) marginal cost pricing conditions; each trading post should cover its costs through the difference in goods bought (at bid price) and sold (at ask price).

The budget balance requirement applies at each transaction at each trading post. Thus, a household acquiring good $j$ for $i$ at $\{i, j\}$ and retrading $j$ at $\{j, k\}$ is acquiring $j$ at its ask price (in terms of $i$) at $\{i, j\}$ and delivering $j$ at its bid price (in terms of $k$) at $\{j, k\}$. In that sequence of trades, the trader experiences − and pays − $j$'s bid−ask spread.

## 6  MONETARY EQUILIBRIUM

Market-clearing bid prices appear in Table 4.1. Each entry represents the bid price of the column good in units of the row good. In this array, good $m$ − with the narrowest prevailing bid−ask spread − is the most liquid (saleable) good, Menger's candidate for commodity money.

**Example 4.1**  The array of equilibrium trades follows:

For $i = 1, 2, 3, 4, \ldots, N; j \neq m,$

$$s_i^{o[i,j]\{i,m\}} = 1, b_m^{o[i,j]\{i,m\}} = 1, s_m^{o[i,j]\{j,m\}} = 1, b_j^{o[i,j]\{j,m\}} = 1 - \delta.$$

For $i = 1, \ldots, N; j = m,$

$$s_i^{o[i,j]\{i,m\}} = 1, b_m^{o[i,j]\{i,m\}} = 1.$$

For $i = m, j = 1, 2, \ldots, m,$

$$s_m^{o[m,j]\{m,j\}} = 1, b_j^{o[m,j]\{m,j\}} = 1 - \delta.$$

The arrangement is a market-clearing equilibrium with all trade going through good $m$. Good $m$ acts as the medium of exchange, commodity money. The trading posts dealing in good $m$, $\{m, 1\}$, $\{m, 2\}$, $\{m, 3\}$,

*Table 4.1  Monetary equilibrium marginal cost pricing – market-clearing bid prices at trading posts*

| Selling: | 1 | 2 | 3 | $\ldots$ | $m$ | $\ldots$ | $N-1$ | $N$ |
|---|---|---|---|---|---|---|---|---|
| **Buying:** | | | | | | | | |
| 1 | X | $(1-\delta)^2$ | $(1-\delta)^2$ | $(1-\delta)^2$ | $(1-\delta)$ | $(1-\delta)^2$ | $(1-\delta)^2$ | $(1-\delta)^2$ |
| 2 | $(1-\delta)^2$ | X | $(1-\delta)^2$ | $(1-\delta)^2$ | $(1-\delta)$ | $(1-\delta)^2$ | $(1-\delta)^2$ | $(1-\delta)^2$ |
| 3 | $(1-\delta)^2$ | $(1-\delta)^2$ | X | $(1-\delta)^2$ | $(1-\delta)$ | $(1-\delta)^2$ | $(1-\delta)^2$ | $(1-\delta)^2$ |
| $\ldots$ | $(1-\delta)^2$ | $(1-\delta)^2$ | $(1-\delta)^2$ | X | $(1-\delta)$ | $(1-\delta)^2$ | $(1-\delta)^2$ | $(1-\delta)^2$ |
| $m$ | 1 | 1 | 1 | 1 | X | 1 | 1 | 1 |
| $\ldots$ | $(1-\delta)^2$ | $(1-\delta)^2$ | $(1-\delta)^2$ | $(1-\delta)^2$ | $(1-\delta)$ | X | $(1-\delta)^2$ | $(1-\delta)^2$ |
| $N-1$ | $(1-\delta)^2$ | $(1-\delta)^2$ | $(1-\delta)^2$ | $(1-\delta)^2$ | $(1-\delta)$ | $(1-\delta)^2$ | X | $(1-\delta)^2$ |
| $N$ | $(1-\delta)^2$ | $(1-\delta)^2$ | $(1-\delta)^2$ | $(1-\delta)^2$ | $(1-\delta)$ | $(1-\delta)^2$ | $(1-\delta)^2$ | X |

. . ., $\{m, N\}$, cover their operating costs. For each good $n = 1, 2, 3,. . .,$ $N, n \neq m$ they find $\Omega$ sellers coming to the post delivering one unit of $n$ in exchange for $m$, and $\Omega$ buyers coming to the post, exchanging good $m$ for good $n$. The trading post clears.

Household $[i, j]$, $(i \neq m \neq j)$ for example, wants to trade good $i$ for good $j$. It considers trading the goods directly at $\{i, j\}$. Pricing at $\{i, j\}$ means that household $[i, j]$ could deliver good $i$ to $\{i, j\}$ and receive good $j$ after incurring a $2\delta - \delta^2$ discount covering the bid—ask spread, using direct trade. Alternatively, $[i, j]$ can trade at $\{i, m\}$ and at $\{j, m\}$. It sells $i$ at $\{i, m\}$ in exchange for $m$ and sells $m$ at $\{j, m\}$ in exchange for the $j$ it really wants. In this indirect trade, it incurs a $\delta$ discount, saving $\delta - \delta^2$ compared to direct trade, by using monetary trade with good $m$ as 'money'. Indirect monetary trade is more attractive because it is less expensive. The lower expense reflects lower resource costs due to the low transaction cost of good $m$ and the matching of suppliers and demanders of each good $n = 1, 2, . . ., N,$ $n \neq m$, at the trading posts $\{m, n\}$ where good $m$ is traded. As Jevons (1875) reminds us, the common medium of exchange overcomes the absence of a double coincidence of wants. Thus each household needs to incur the transaction cost on only one side of the monetary trade it enters.

In equilibrium, all trading posts $\{i, j\}$, $i, j \neq m$, except those dealing in good $m$ become inactive. All trading posts are priced, but trade is transacted only at the $N - 1$ posts dealing in $m$. The trading posts clear. Good $m$ has become the common medium of exchange, commodity money.

# 7  CONCLUSION

There is a surprise here. Tobin (1961, 1980) and Hahn (1982) despaired of achieving a general equilibrium model based on elementary price theory resulting in a common medium of exchange. But the price array in Table 4.1 leads directly to a monetary equilibrium. Monetary trade is the result of decentralized optimizing decisions of households guided by prices without government, central direction, or fiat. The price system provides all the coordination required to maintain a common medium of exchange. Of course, we expect successful decentralized coordination in an Arrow—Debreu Walrasian general equilibrium model (Debreu, 1959). But the Arrow—Debreu model is framed for a nonmonetary economy. The example here demonstrates − as Menger (1892) argued − that the price system can generate a monetary equilibrium with a single common medium of exchange.

## NOTES

1.  This chapter is based on Starr (2008a).
2.  See Radford (1945) on the evolution of a cigarette currency and Newhouse (2004) on convergence to monetary equilibrium in a 3-commodity model. Banerjee and Maskin (1996) focus on the ease or difficulty of assessing quality – a form of saleableness – as the rationale for a common medium of exchange.

# 5. Absence of double coincidence of wants is essential to monetization in a linear economy[1]

Following the model of Chapter 4, this chapter again considers a pure exchange trading post economy with linear transaction costs, and a range of transaction costs for the various commodities. Bid and ask prices for all goods in exchange for the low transaction cost good reflect its low transaction cost, creating a narrow bid—ask spread. In general equilibrium and assuming the absence of double coincidence of wants, the low transaction cost commodity becomes the common medium of exchange. Conversely, in the presence of double coincidence of wants, assuming positive linear transaction costs for all goods, there is a barter equilibrium and no monetary equilibrium. Hence, in a linear model, absence of double coincidence of wants is a necessary condition for the existence of monetary equilibrium.

## 1 DOUBLE COINCIDENCE OF WANTS

In this chapter, we shall use again Chapter 4's model of segmented markets with linear transaction costs. We shall consider two variants: absence of double coincidence of wants with variation in transaction costs among goods; and full double coincidence of wants. In the first case, commodity money (the low transaction cost good) arises endogenously in market equilibrium. In the second case there is a barter equilibrium and no monetary equilibrium. Thus, this last case demonstrates — in a linear model — that the absence of double coincidence of wants is essential to monetization of trade. It does so by considering the same problem with full double coincidence of wants and finding that the result is necessarily a nonmonetary equilibrium.

## 2   THE LOW TRANSACTION COST INSTRUMENT IS 'MONEY'

This chapter reproduces and expands Chapter 4's model. Separate bid and ask prices represent transaction costs and put a price on liquidity: a good's bid—ask spread is the price of using it as a medium of exchange. Hence, a good with a uniformly narrow bid—ask spread is highly liquid — in Menger's word 'saleable' — and constitutes a natural 'money'. Price theory implies monetary theory. Liquidity creates monetization.

Starting from the nonmonetary Arrow—Debreu model, two additional structures are sufficient to give endogenous monetization in equilibrium: multiple budget constraints (one at each transaction, not just on net trade) and transaction costs. One way of formalizing multiple budget constraints is a trading post model. Thus, if there are $N$ goods actively traded, there are $\frac{1}{2}N(N-1)$ possible trading posts. That is the starting point of the examples below. The choice of which trading posts a typical household will trade at is part of the household optimization. The equilibrium structure of exchange is the array of trading posts that actually host active trade. The determination of which trading posts are active in equilibrium is endogenous to the model and characterizes the monetary character of trade. The equilibrium is monetary with a unique money if only $(N-1)$ trading posts are active, those trading all goods against 'money'.

## 3   MONETIZATION COMES FROM LIQUIDITY: MONETARY COMPETITIVE EQUILIBRIUM WITH LINEAR TRANSACTION COSTS

The distinctive features of the model were presented in Chapter 3, summarized as the trading post balance constraints: (i) transactions exchange pairs of goods, and (ii) budget constraints are enforced at each transaction separately, generating a role for a carrier of value between transactions (a medium of exchange). In this chapter, (iii) transaction costs are assumed to be linear and positive (unlike good $m$'s zero transaction cost in Chapter 4). In the linear transaction cost case without double coincidence of wants, the most liquid (lowest transaction cost) good becomes the common medium of exchange. There may be multiple media of exchange when there is a tie for lowest cost.

Let there be $N$ commodities, numbered 1, 2, . . ., $N$. They are traded in pairs — good $i$ for good $j$ — at specialized trading posts. The trading post for trade of good $i$ versus good $j$ (and vice versa) is designated $\{i, j\}$;

trading post $\{i, j\}$ is the same trading post as $\{j, i\}$. Trading post $\{i, j\}$ is a business firm, the market maker in trade between goods $i$ and $j$. $\{i, j\}$ actively buys and (re)sells both $i$ and $j$. Trade as a resource-using activity is modeled by describing the post's transaction costs. The notion of transaction cost summarizes costs that in an actual economy are incurred by retailers, wholesalers, individual firms and households. The bid–ask spread summarizes these costs to the model's transactors. Thus, part of transaction cost represents the (nonmarketed) time and resources used by households in arranging their transactions, summarized here imprecisely as a price spread.[2]

The transaction cost function for trading post $\{i, j\}$ is:

$$C^{\{i,j\}} = \delta^i y_i^{\{i,j\}B} + \delta^j y_j^{\{i,j\}B} \quad \text{(TCL)} \tag{5.1}$$

where $\delta^i, \delta^j > 0$. In words, the transaction technology looks like this. Trading post $\{i, j\}$ makes a market in goods $i$ and $j$, buying each good in order to resell it. It incurs transaction costs in the same goods. These costs vary directly (in proportions $\delta^i, \delta^j$ ) with volume of trade. The transaction cost structure is separable in the two principal traded goods. The transaction cost function $C^{\{i,j\}}$ is sufficiently flexible to distinguish transaction costs differing among commodities, including differences in durability, portability, and recognizability.

The population of trading households is just as in Chapter 4. Consider a pure exchange trading post economy with $N$ commodities, $N \geq 3$. $\Omega$ denotes the greatest integer $\leq (N - 1)/2$.

Let $[i, j]$ denote a household endowed with good $i$ that prefers good $j$; $i \neq j, i, j = 1, 2, \ldots, N$. Household $[i, j]$'s endowment is 1 unit of commodity $i$. Denote the endowment of [i, j] as $r_i^{[i,j]} = A$. $[i, j]$'s utility function is $u^{[i,j]}(x_1, x_2, x_3, \ldots, x_N) = x_j$. That is, household $[i, j]$ values good $j$ only. It cares for $i$ only as a resource to trade for $j$. This is obviously an immense oversimplification — but it serves to focus the issue.

Consider a population denoted $\Theta$ of households including $\Omega$ households endowed with each good and each household desiring a good different from its endowment. There are $\Omega$ households endowed with good 1, preferring respectively, goods 2, 3, 4, . . ., $\Omega + 1$: [1, 2], [1, 3], [1, 4], . . ., [1, $\Omega + 1$]. There are $\Omega$ households endowed with good 2, preferring respectively goods 3, 4, 5, . . ., $\Omega + 2$: [2, 3], [2, 4], [2, 5], . . ., [2, $\Omega + 2$]. The roll call of households proceeds through [$N$, 1], [$N$, 2], [$N$, 3], . . ., [$N$, $\Omega$].

One way to think of $\Theta$ is that its elements $[i, j]$ are set round a clock-face at a position corresponding to the endowed good, $i$, eager to acquire $j$, $j$ being 1, 2, . . ., $\Omega$, steps clockwise from $i$. Population $\Theta$ displays absence of double coincidence of wants. For each household endowed with good $i$ and desiring good $j$, $[i, j]$, there is no precise mirror image, $[j, i]$. Nevertheless, there are $\Omega$ households endowed with one unit of commodity 1, and $\Omega$ households strongly preferring commodity 1 to all others. That is true for each good. Thus gross supplies equal gross demands, though there is no immediate opportunity for any two households to make a mutually advantageous trade. Jevons (1875) tells us that this is precisely the setting where money is suitable to facilitate trade.

The bid prices (the prices at which the trading post will buy from households) at $\{i,j\}$ are $q_i^{\{i,j\}}$, $q_j^{\{i,j\}}$ for goods $i$ and $j$, respectively. The price of $i$ is in units of $j$. The price of $j$ is in units of $i$. The ask price (the price at which the trading post will sell to households) of $j$ is the inverse of the bid price of $i$ (and vice versa). That is, $(q_i^{\{i,j\}})^{-1}$ and $(q_j^{\{i,j\}})^{-1}$ are the ask prices of $j$ and $i$ at $\{i,j\}$. The trading post $\{i,j\}$ covers its costs by the difference between the bid and ask prices of $i$ and $j$, that is, by the spread $(q_j^{\{i,j\}})^{-1} - q_i^{\{i,j\}}$ and the spread $(q_i^{\{i,j\}})^{-1} - q_j^{\{i,j\}}$.

Given $q_i^{\{i,j\}}, q_j^{\{i,j\}}$, for all $\{i,j\}$, household $h$ then forms its buying and selling plans, in particular deciding which trading posts to use to execute its desired trades. Household $h \in \Theta$ faces the following trading post balance constraints enunciated in Chapter 3:

(T.i) $b_n^{h\{i,j\}} > 0$ only if $n = i,j$; $s_n^{h\{i,j\}} > 0$ only if $n = i,j$.

(T.ii) $b_i^{h\{i,j\}} \leq q_j^{\{i,j\}} \cdot s_j^{h\{i,j\}}$, $b_j^{h\{i,j\}} \leq q_i^{\{i,j\}} \cdot s_i^{h\{i,j\}}$ for each $\{i,j\}$.

(T.iii) $x_n^h = r_n^h + \Sigma_{\{i,j\}} b_n^{h\{i,j\}} - \Sigma_{\{i,j\}} s_n^{h\{i,j\}} \geq 0, 0 \leq n \leq N$.

Note that condition (T.ii) defines a budget balance requirement at the transaction level, implying the decentralized character of trade. Since the budget constraint applies to each pairwise transaction separately, there may be a demand for a carrier of value to move purchasing power between distinct transactions. $h$ faces the array of bid prices $q_i^{\{i,j\}}, q_j^{\{i,j\}}$ and chooses $s_n^{h\{i,j\}}$ and $b_n^{h\{i,j\}}$, $n = i,j$, to maximize $u^h(x^h)$ subject to (T.i), (T.ii), (T.iii). That is, $h$ chooses which pairwise markets to transact in and a transaction plan to optimize utility, subject to a multiplicity of pairwise budget constraints. The trading posts have linear transaction technologies. A competitive equilibrium is an appropriate solution concept resulting in zero profits for the typical trading post (with the additional benefit that no account need be taken of distribution of profits). The threat of entry (by other similar trading post firms) rationalizes the competitive model, but for simplicity we take there to be a unique trading post firm making a market in goods $i$ and $j$, denoted indiscriminately $\{i,j\} = \{j,i\}$.

As described in Chapter 3, a competitive equilibrium under (TCL) consists of $q_i^{o\{i,j\}}, q_j^{o\{i,j\}}$, $1 \leq i,j \leq N$, so that:

- For each household $h \in \Theta$, there is a utility-optimizing plan $b_n^{oh\{i,j\}}$, $s_n^{oh\{i,j\}}$ (subject to T.i, T.ii, T.iii) so that $\Sigma_h b_n^{oh\{i,j\}} = y_n^{o\{i,j\}S}$, $\Sigma_h s_n^{oh\{i,j\}} = y_n^{o\{i,j\}B}$, $n = i, j$, for each $\{i,j\}$, each $n$, where
- $y_n^{o\{i,j\}S} \leq y_n^{o\{i,j\}B}$, $n = i, j$.
- $\delta^i y_i^{o\{i,j\}B} + \delta^j y_j^{o\{i,j\}B} = y_i^{o\{i,j\}B} + y_j^{o\{i,j\}B} - y_i^{o\{i,j\}S} - y_j^{o\{i,j\}S}$.

# 4 MONETARY EQUILIBRIUM

Jevons (1875) reminds us that monetization of trade follows in part from the absence of a double coincidence of wants. In the present model, that logic is particularly powerful. Absence of coincidence of wants means that the typical traded good will be traded more than once in moving from endowment to consumption. Barter trade successfully rearranging the allocation to an equilibrium will transact an endowment first at the trading post where it is supplied and again at a distinct post where it is demanded. Hence monetary trade as an alternative (substituting retrade of money for the retrade of nonmonetary goods) can be undertaken without increasing total trading volume or transaction cost, even without scale economies. Conversely, when there is a full double coincidence of wants and linear transaction cost, equilibrium will be nonmonetary even in the presence of a natural money.

**Example 5.1** (Existence of monetary equilibrium with a most liquid asset, absent double coincidence of wants) Let the population of households be $\Theta$. Let $C^{\{i,j\}}$ be described by (TCL). Let $0 < \delta^m < \delta^i$, for $i = 1, 2, 3, \ldots, m - 1, m + 1, \ldots, N, i \neq m$. Transaction costs are constant and nontrivial for all goods; they are significantly lower in good $m$. Then there is a unique competitive equilibrium allocation (though a range of prices may support the *unique* real allocation of trades and consumptions). The equilibrium is a monetary equilibrium with good $m$ as the unique 'money'. The notation $\oplus$ is defined in the following way. For any $n, j = 1, 2, \ldots, N$, $n \oplus j \equiv n + j$ if $n + j \leq N$, or $\equiv n + j - N$ if $n + j > N$. That is, $n \oplus j$ is $n + j \bmod N$.

**Demonstration of Example 5.1**   Using marginal cost pricing and market clearing, we have for each $\{i,j\}, i \neq j, m \neq i, j; 1 \leq i, j \leq N, k = 1, 2, \ldots, \Omega$,

$$q_{i \oplus k}^{\{i, i \oplus k\}} = 1, \quad q_i^{\{i, i \oplus k\}} = \frac{1 - \delta^i}{1 + \delta^{i \oplus k}},$$

and for

$$j \neq i, i \oplus k, q_i^{\{i,j\}} = 1 - \delta^i; q_i^{\{i,m\}} = \frac{1 - \delta^i}{1 + \delta^m}, q_1^{\{i,m\}} = 1.$$

$$s_i^{[i,i\oplus k]\{i,m\}} = A, \ b_1^{[i,i\oplus k]\{i,m\}} = q_i^{\{i,m\}} A = s_m^{[i,i\oplus k]\{i\oplus k,m\}}, \ b_{i\oplus k}^{[i,i\oplus k]\{i\oplus k,m\}} = q_i^{\{i,m\}} q_m^{\{i\oplus m,m\}} A.$$

What is happening in Example 5.1? At first household $[i, i \oplus k]$ goes to trading post $\{i, i \oplus k\}$ offering $i$ in exchange for $i \oplus k$. But no one is coming to the trading post offering $i \oplus k$. So good $i$ is priced at a large discount at the post, reflecting the transaction costs of both $i$ and $i \oplus k$. On all other markets $\{i, j\}$ goods are priced to reflect their transaction costs, $q_i^{\{i,j\}} = 1 - \delta^i$. But at that pricing, since $\delta^m < \delta^i$, it is advantageous for $[i, i \oplus k]$ to trade through $m$ as an intermediary. This follows since $(1 - \delta^i) \cdot (1 - \delta^m) > (1 - \delta^i) \cdot (1 - \delta^{i \oplus k})$. This pricing creates a small shortage of $m$ at each trading post (since small quantities of $m$ are being retained at the post to cover $m$'s transaction costs) so prices are readjusted so that all of the discount in bid prices at $\{i, m\}$ appears in the bid price of $i$. This results in $q_i^{\{i,1\}} = \frac{1 - \delta^i}{1 + \delta^m}$, $q_m^{\{i,m\}} = 1$. All trade of $i$ for $i \oplus k$ now goes through $m$. Good $m$ has become 'money', the unique low transaction cost common medium of exchange.

In actual monetary economies we usually see a single 'money' as in Example 5.1. We shall argue in Chapter 6 that the reason for uniqueness of 'money' is scale economy. Does there have to be a reason for uniqueness? Yes. US dollars, pounds sterling, and euros, all have similar low transaction costs but in their separate markets they are virtually unique in use. Economic theory should have an explanation for this uniqueness. Example 5.2 below emphasizes, by counterexample, that the nonconvexity in Chapter 6 is important. In Example 5.2, absent the nonconvexity, when there is a tie for lowest transaction cost, there are many media of exchange in use. Is a tie realistic; is it not a singularity? The example of dollars, sterling, and euros suggests that on the contrary, the notion of a tie for lowest transaction cost is a nontrivial event, so that uniqueness requires an explanation.

**Example 5.2** (Multiple 'moneys' in equilibrium) Let the population of households be $\Theta$. Let $C^{\{i,j\}}$ be described by TCL. Let $0 < \delta^\mu = \delta^\nu = \delta^\kappa < \delta^i < 1/3$, $i = 1, 2, 3, \ldots, N$, $i \neq \mu, \nu, \kappa$. Then there is a continuum of competitive equilibrium allocations with $\mu, \nu, \kappa$ acting as 'money' in proportions from 0 to 100 percent. Consumptions and utilities of all households are the same as in the equilibrium of Example 5.1.

**Demonstration of Example 5.2** The marginal cost market-clearing pricing is identical to that in Example 5.1 with goods $\mu, \nu, \kappa$ priced similarly to good $m$. The exception is trade between 'moneys' where $q_\mu^{\{\mu,\nu\}} = 1 - \delta^\mu$, and similarly for $\nu, \kappa$, all of these bid prices being equal. The trading posts $\{i, \mu\}, \{i, \nu\}$, and $\{i, \kappa\}, 1 \le i \le N, i \neq \mu, \nu, \kappa$ (for trade in good $i$ versus goods $\mu, \nu, \kappa$ ) are the trading posts with narrow bid−ask spreads since $\mu, \nu, \kappa$ have low transaction costs. Households can now divide their transactions among trading posts for goods $\mu, \nu, \kappa$ versus all other goods in any proportion (though in equilibrium they will be the same proportions for all households). Markets clear.

The logic of Example 5.2 is merely the multi-money version of 5.1. Goods $\mu, \nu, \kappa$ are equally liquid and become media of exchange. They can be used, however, in any proportionate combination from 0 to 100 percent since absent economies of scale there is no reason further to specialize.

# 5 ABSENCE OF DOUBLE COINCIDENCE OF WANTS IS ESSENTIAL TO MONETIZATION IN A LINEAR MODEL

Let $\Theta^D = \{[m, n] | m, n = 1, 2, 3, \ldots, N, m \neq n\}$. $\Theta^D$ is distinctive in creating a population of households with fully complementary demands and supplies, full double coincidence of wants. We can use this population to illustrate the importance of the absence of double coincidence of wants to monetization in a linear model. Under the same conditions where monetary equilibria existed − and indeed were the only equilibria − in Examples 5.1 and 5.2 in the absence of double coincidence of wants, we can show that for $\Theta^D$, with full double coincidence of wants, a barter equilibrium is the unique competitive equilibrium. Hence the classical focus on the absence of double coincidence of wants is confirmed; it is essential to monetization in a linear model. Note that this result depends on the linearity (or convexity) of transaction costs; if scale economies are present, then even with full double coincidence of wants, it may be more economical to use a common medium of exchange with resulting high trading volumes.

**Example 5.3** (Barter equilibrium with full double coincidence of wants) Let the population of households be $\Theta^D$. Let $C^{\{i,j\}}$ be described by (TCL). Let $0 < \delta^m < \delta^i$, for all $i \neq m, i = 1, 2, 3, \ldots, N$. Transaction costs are constant and nontrivial for all goods but $m$. Then there is a unique competitive equilibrium allocation. The equilibrium is nonmonetary with active trade in all trading posts $\{i, j\}, 1 \le i, j \le N$.

**Demonstration of Example 5.3** For each $i, j, 1 \le i, j \le N, q_i^{\{i,j\}} = (1 - \delta^i)$, $q_j^{\{i,j\}} = (1 - \delta^j)$. $s_i^{[i,j]\{i,j\}} = A, b_j^{[i,j]\{i,j\}} = q_i^{\{i,j\}}A, s_j^{[j,i]\{i,j\}} = A, b_i^{[j,i]\{i,j\}} = q_j^{\{i,j\}}A$. Markets clear. The allocation is an equilibrium.

What is happening in Example 5.3? Direct barter trade works successfully in the presence of double coincidence of wants. For each household $[i, j]$ with a supply of one good and a demand for another, there is a precise mirror image $[j, i]$ in the population. They each go to the trading post $\{i, j\}$ where their common demands and supplies are traded. They trade, each incurring the cost of trading one good. Monetary trade is not advantageous since it requires twice the transactions volume − with corresponding cost − of direct barter trade (similar volumes for each nonmonetary good and an equal volume of trade in the medium of exchange). Monetization of trade in equilibrium in a *linear model* depends on absence of double coincidence of wants.

## 6    CONCLUSION

The examples of this chapter provide a very general treatment for the case of linear transaction costs. They demonstrate what Jevons (1875) taught us and economists have known for centuries. A 'natural money', a lowest transaction cost good, will become the common medium of exchange when there is an absence of double coincidence of wants. But they say something more.

In a linear model, when there are several 'natural moneys', there will be several common media of exchange. But how then do we explain the observation of Chapter 1, that money is (locally) unique; money differs among economies, but almost all the transactions in most places most of the time use a single common medium of exchange? A usage so universal should have a universal explanation.

In a linear model, when double coincidence of wants occurs, barter is preferable to monetary trade. This seems obvious. But how then do we explain the observation of Chapter 1, that even transactions displaying a double coincidence of wants are transacted with money? That is a puzzle.

The resolution to these challenges is proposed in Chapter 6. The model should not be linear. There is a scale economy. Money is a natural monopoly; in equilibrium it will be unique.

## NOTES

1.   This chapter is based on Starr (2003, 2004).
2.   An alternative more explicit treatment of household nonmarket transaction cost decisions is embodied in Kurz (1974).

# 6. Uniqueness of money: scale economy and network externality[1]

Uniqueness of the medium of exchange and the use of monetary trade even in the presence of double coincidence of wants is explained by scale economies in transaction costs. A network externality encourages all transactions to proceed through the single common medium of exchange.

## 1 UNIQUENESS OF THE MEDIUM OF EXCHANGE: SCALE ECONOMIES IN TRANSACTION COST

Monetary trade is typically characterized by a unique medium of exchange or a small number of related media (for example, currency, credit cards, travelers' checks, all denominated in US$). How does this come about? Tobin (1980, p. 86) suggests that scale economies and a network externality in transaction costs are essential:

> The use of a particular language or a particular money by one individual increases its value to other actual or potential users. Increasing returns to scale . . . explains the tendency for one basic language or money to monopolize the field.

When monetization takes place, households supplying good $i$ and demanding good $j$ are induced to trade in a monetary fashion, first trading $i$ for 'money' and then 'money' for $j$, by discovering that transaction costs are lower in this indirect trade than in direct trade of $i$ for $j$. But as Example 5.2 points out, monetization of trade is no guarantee of uniqueness of the medium of exchange.

Scale economies in transaction costs induce specialization in the medium of exchange function. High volume leads to low unit transaction costs (see also Howitt and Clower, 2000, Rey, 2001 and Starr and Stinchcombe, 1999). Scale economy is not a necessary condition for uniqueness of the medium of exchange in equilibrium (Example 4.1), but scale economy helps to ensure uniqueness (Example 6.1, below). If there are many equally low-cost candidates for the medium of exchange, then scale economy in transaction costs will allow one to be endogenously chosen as the unique medium of exchange.

This chapter investigates nonconvex transaction costs — that is, a scale economy (indeed an unbounded scale economy) in transaction cost. Scale economy is inconsistent with the existence of a competitive equilibrium. Competitive equilibria typically cannot exist in the unbounded scale economy environment. Posit, instead, average cost pricing equilibrium. The use of average cost pricing is subject to interpretation. A literal interpretation is that there is a natural monopoly market-maker pricing at average cost to discourage new entry. An alternative is that the operation of the market is in the nature of a public good; the nonconvex technology is a summary of the interactions of many individual agents sharing an economy of scale, and hence average cost pricing reflects the common benefit from the level of activity in the market (a Marshallian externality).

Hahn (1997) comments that in the presence of market set-up costs, each transactor in the market benefits from the participation of others: 'If the number who can gain from trade is . . . sufficiently [large], the Pareto improving trade will take place. There is thus an externality induced by set-up costs'. Young (1998) assumes the externality without additional explanation. Rey (2001) denotes this interaction the 'thick markets externality'. Thus, in this setting, the scale economy takes the form of reductions in the bid—ask spread faced by all transactors in proportion to the number of active transactions. It is a network externality.

This chapter introduces a relatively narrow class of examples. The cost function (TCNC) and trading populations are very specific — though we hope the results will generalize. Why this rush to specificity? Why concentrate on examples, rather than develop general results, comparable in their generality to the Arrow—Debreu model? Large nonconvexities — large enough to create a natural monopoly — constitute a real modeling problem. Intuitions are clear and examples abound, but it is very hard to generate general results. Hence the reliance on a class of examples.

If transaction costs reflect a scale economy, characterized by (TCNC), the issue is more nuanced. The scale economy suggests a natural monopoly. But the economic issue here is more complex. The transaction costs here portrayed at the level of the trading post (for modeling precision and convenience) are in actual economies incurred at households, firms — some explicitly paid, others internalized. For these reasons, we shall portray pricing as an average cost process. The notion here is that the transaction cost structure is modeling a network externality.

Scale economy implies a cost saving resulting from uniqueness of 'money', since only $N - 1$ trading posts need to operate at positive volume, incurring significantly lower costs than the $\frac{1}{2}N(N - 1)$ posts possible in a barter equilibrium. Scale economies make it cost saving to concentrate transactions in a few trading posts and one intermediary instrument.

## 2 MONETIZATION COMES FROM LIQUIDITY AGAIN: MONETARY GENERAL EQUILIBRIUM WITH UNIQUE MONEY UNDER AVERAGE COST PRICING OF NONCONVEX TRANSACTION COSTS

Scale economies in the transaction cost structure induce uniqueness of the equilibrium medium of exchange. 'Money' is a natural monopoly. As Tobin (1959, p. 35) asks: 'Why are some assets selected by a society as generally acceptable media of exchange while others are not? This is not an easy question, because the selection is self-justifying'. In the language of general equilibrium theory, 'self-justifying' means that a successful self-reinforcing choice of the common medium of exchange is a fixed point. Thus gold and dollar bills may have low transaction costs and be excellent candidates for a medium of exchange, but if (despite high transaction cost) cigarettes are already the commonly chosen medium of exchange with high trading volume, then cigarettes may have the lowest average transaction cost. The choice of cigarettes as the common medium of exchange is then 'self-justifying'.

The nonconvex (scale economy) cost function for trading post $\{i,j\}$ is:

$$C^{\{i,j\}} = \min[\delta^i y_i^{\{i,j\}B}, \gamma^i] + \min[\delta^j y_j^{\{i,j\}B}, \gamma^j] \quad \text{(TCNC)} \qquad (6.1)$$

where $\delta^i, \delta^j, \gamma^i, \gamma^j > 0$. In words, the transaction technology looks like this: trading post $\{i,j\}$ makes a market in goods $i$ and $j$, buying each good in order to resell it. It incurs transaction costs. These costs vary directly (in proportions $\delta^i, \delta^j$) with volume of trade at low volume and then hit a ceiling after which they do not increase with trading volume. The specification in (TCNC) is an extreme case: zero marginal transaction cost beyond the ceiling. Adding additional linear terms would represent a more general case.

Since the trading posts in this economy have nonconvex transaction technologies, a competitive equilibrium is not an appropriate solution concept. The equilibrium notion used is an average cost pricing equilibrium resulting in zero profits for the typical trading post firm.

An average cost pricing equilibrium consists of $q_i^{o\{i,j\}}, q_j^{o\{i,j\}}, 1 \leq i,j \leq N$, so that:

- For each household $h$, there is a utility-optimizing plan $b_n^{oh\{i,j\}}$, $s_n^{oh\{i,j\}}$ (subject to T.i, T.ii, T.iii) so that $\Sigma_h b_n^{oh\{i,j\}} = y_n^{o\{i,j\}S}$, $\Sigma_h s_n^{oh\{i,j\}} = y_n^{o\{i,j\}B}$, for each $\{i,j\}$, each $n$, where:
- $y_n^{o\{i,j\}S} \le y_n^{o\{i,j\}B}$, $n = i,j$.
- $C^{o\{i,j\}} = y_j^{o\{i,j\}B} - y_j^{o\{i,j\}S} - y_i^{o\{i,j\}S} + y_i^{o\{i,j\}B}$

The population of trading households is similar to that of Chapter 4. Consider a pure exchange trading post economy with $N$ commodities, $N \ge 3$. $\Omega$ denotes the greatest integer $\le (N-1)/2$.

[$i, j$] denotes a household endowed with good $i$ that prefers good $j$; $i \ne j$, $i, j = 1, 2, \ldots, N$. [$i, j$]'s endowment is $A$ units of commodity $i$, denoted $r_i^{[i,j]} = A$. [$i, j$]'s utility function is $u^{[i,j]}(x_1, x_2, x_3, \ldots, x_N) = x_j$. That is, household [$i, j$] values good $j$ only. It cares for $i$ only as a resource to trade for $j$. This is obviously an immense oversimplification − but it serves to focus the issue.

Just as in Chapter 4, consider a population denoted $\Theta$ of households including $\Omega$ households endowed with each good and each household desiring a good different from its endowment. There are $\Omega$ households endowed with good 1, preferring respectively, goods 2, 3, 4, . . ., $\Omega + 1$: [1, 2], [1, 3], [1, 4], . . ., [1, $\Omega + 1$]. There are $\Omega$ households endowed with good 2, preferring respectively, goods 3, 4, 5, . . ., $\Omega + 2$: [2, 3], [2, 4], [2, 5], . . ., [2, $\Omega + 2$]. The roll call of households proceeds through [$N$, 1], [$N$, 2], [$N$, 3], . . ., [$N$, $\Omega$].

Just as in Chapter 4, one way to think of $\Theta$ is that its elements [$i, j$] are set round a clock-face at a position corresponding to the endowed good, $i$, eager to acquire $j$, $j$ being 1, 2, . . ., $\Omega$, steps clockwise from $i$. Population $\Theta$ displays absence of double coincidence of wants. For each household endowed with good $i$ and desiring good $j$, [$i, j$], there is no precise mirror image, [$j, i$]. Nevertheless, there are $\Omega$ households endowed with $A$ of commodity $i$, and $\Omega$ households strongly preferring commodity $i$ to all others. That is true for each good. Thus gross supplies equal gross demands, though there is no immediate opportunity for any two households to make a mutually advantageous trade. Jevons (1875) tells us that this is precisely the setting where money is suitable to facilitate trade. Around the clock-face, households could arrange a Pareto-improving redistribution by each taking its endowment and sending it $|i - j|$ places counterclockwise. However, reflecting the absence of double coincidence of wants, if each of the households in $\Theta$ goes to the trading post where its endowment is traded against its desired good, it finds itself alone. It is dealing on a thin market. The following Example 6.1 demonstrates that, with scale economies in transaction cost, virtually any good can become money; the designation is self-confirming, just as Tobin suggested.

**Example 6.1** (Monetary equilibrium absent double coincidence of wants with scale economy in transaction costs) Let the population of households be $\Theta$. Let $C^{\{i,j\}}$ be described by (TCNC). Let $0 < \delta^j < 1$ for all $j = 1, 2, \ldots, N$. Let there be $i^*$ so that $(1 - \frac{\gamma^{i^*} + \gamma^j}{\Omega A}) > (1 - \delta^j)$ for all $i^* \neq j$, $j = 1, 2, \ldots, N$. Then for each such $i^*$ there is a monetary average cost pricing equilibrium with good $i^*$ as the unique 'money'.

**Demonstration of Example 6.1** The average cost pricing equilibrium price array is shown in Table 6.1. There may be more than one $i^*$ fulfilling the inequalities above. Choose one $i^*$ arbitrarily as 'money'.

For all $j \neq i^*$, $j = 1, 2, \ldots, N$, let $q_{i^*}^{\{i^*,j\}} = 1$, $q_j^{\{i^*,j\}} = 1 - \frac{\gamma^{i^*} + \gamma^j}{\Omega A}$.
For all $j$, and $k = 1, 2, \ldots, N$, $j \neq k \neq i^*$, $q_j^{\{j,k\}} = 1 - \delta^j$, $q_k^{\{j,k\}} = 1 - \delta^k$.
For $1 \leq \ell \leq \Omega$, let $s_m^{[m,m\oplus\ell]\{i^*,m\}} = A$, $b_{i^*}^{[m,m\oplus\ell]\{i^*,m\}} = q_m^{\{i^*,m\}}A$,
$s_{i^*}^{[m,m\oplus\ell]\{i^*,m\oplus\ell\}} = q_m^{\{i^*,m\}}A$, $b_{m\oplus\ell}^{[m,m\oplus\ell]\{i^*,m\oplus\ell\}} = q_m^{\{i^*,m\}}A$.

What is happening in Example 6.1? Virtually any good $i^*$ can become money. Monetization comes from liquidity and $-$ with scale economies $-$ liquidity comes from trading volume. The economy is focusing on good $i^*$ as its common medium of exchange. Since there are scale economies in transaction costs, high trading volume means low average cost with concomitant narrow bid$-$ask spread. The narrow bid$-$ask spread is the way the price system confirms and reinforces the choice of $i^*$ as the medium of exchange. Trader $[m, m \oplus k]$ wants to trade good $m$ for good $m \oplus k$. He could do so directly, but the transaction costs are heavy, reducing his return on the trade to $A(1 - \delta^m)(1 - \delta^{m\oplus k})$ units of $m \oplus k$ after starting with $A$ units of good $m$. The alternative is to trade good $m$ for good $i^*$ and then trade $i^*$ for $m \oplus k$. This results in $A[1 - \frac{\gamma^{i^*} + \gamma^{m\oplus k}}{\Omega A}]$ units of $m\oplus k$. When $\Omega$ is sufficiently large, that is a much greater return. Because of the narrow bid$-$ask spread on trade through $i^*$, every market with good $i^*$ on one side attracts high trading volume, $\Omega$ traders on each side of the market, the high trading volume needed to maintain good $i^*$'s low bid$-$ask spreads. The scale economy means that the choice of good $i^*$ as the common medium of exchange is self-confirming.

The difference between barter and monetary exchange is the contrast between a complex of many thin high transaction cost markets and an array of a smaller number of thick low transaction cost markets dealing in each good versus a unique common medium of exchange. As Tobin claimed, the choice of medium of exchange is self-justifying. Any good $i^*$ with sufficient scale economy in its transaction technology (with $\gamma^{i^*}$, the ceiling on its transaction costs, sufficiently low) can become the unique medium of exchange in equilibrium when trading volume $\Omega A$ is

Table 6.1 *Monetary equilibrium average cost pricing – market-clearing bid prices at trading posts*

| Selling: | 1 | 2 | 3 | ... | $i^*$ | ... | $N-1$ | $N$ |
|---|---|---|---|---|---|---|---|---|
| **Buying:** | | | | | | | | |
| 1 | X | $1-\delta^2$ | $1-\delta^3$ | ... | 1 | ... | $1-\delta^{N-1}$ | $1-\delta^N$ |
| 2 | $1-\delta^1$ | X | $1-\delta^3$ | ... | 1 | ... | $1-\delta^{N-1}$ | $1-\delta^N$ |
| 3 | $1-\delta^1$ | $1-\delta^2$ | X | ... | 1 | ... | $1-\delta^{N-1}$ | $1-\delta^N$ |
| ... | $1-\delta^1$ | $1-\delta^2$ | $1-\delta^3$ | X | 1 | ... | $1-\delta^{N-1}$ | $1-\delta^N$ |
| $i^*$ | $1-\dfrac{\gamma^{i^*}+\gamma^1}{\Omega A}$ | $1-\dfrac{\gamma^{i^*}+\gamma^2}{\Omega A}$ | $1-\dfrac{\gamma^{i^*}+\gamma^3}{\Omega A}$ | ... | X | ... | $1-\dfrac{\gamma^{i^*}+\gamma^{N-1}}{\Omega A}$ | $1-\dfrac{\gamma^{i^*}+\gamma^N}{\Omega A}$ |
| ... | $1-\delta^1$ | $1-\delta^2$ | $1-\delta^3$ | ... | 1 | X | $1-\delta^{N-1}$ | $1-\delta^N$ |
| $N-1$ | $1-\delta^1$ | $1-\delta^2$ | $1-\delta^3$ | ... | 1 | ... | X | $1-\delta^N$ |
| $N$ | $1-\delta^1$ | $1-\delta^2$ | $1-\delta^3$ | ... | 1 | ... | $1-\delta^{N-1}$ | X |

sufficiently high. Mint-standardized gold coins (with a low-cost transaction technology) or cattle (high-cost technology) may be 'money' depending on which is well established. Sufficient trading volume can confirm either choice.

Recall $\Theta^D = \{[m,n]|m,n = 1,2,3,\ldots,N, m \neq n\}$. $\Theta^D$ is distinctive in creating a population of households with fully complementary demands and supplies, full double coincidence of wants. $\Theta^D$ is a set of $N(N-1)$ households with full double coincidence of wants. Example 5.3 established that in a linear transaction cost structure, $\Theta^D$ generates a barter equilibrium. The following Example 6.2 demonstrates, in contrast, that even in the presence of double coincidence of wants, sufficient scale economies in transaction costs can lead to monetization of trade, the use of a common medium of exchange.

**Example 6.2** (Monetary equilibrium with full double coincidence of wants and scale economy in transaction costs) Let the population of households be $\Theta^D$ with $r_i^{[i,j]} = A$. Let $C^{\{i,j\}}$ be described by (TCNC). Let $0 < \delta^i < 1$ all $i = 1,2,\ldots,N$. For some $i*$ and all $j$, $1 \leq i*, j \leq N, i* \neq j$, let $(1 - \frac{\gamma^{i*} + \gamma^j}{(N-1)A}) > (1 - \delta^j)$, $(1 - \frac{\gamma^{i*} + \gamma^j}{(N-1)A}) > (1 - \delta^{i*})$. Then there is a monetary average cost pricing equilibrium with good $i*$ as the unique 'money'.

**Demonstration of Example 6.2** The average cost equilibrium pricing array is presented in Table 6.2. For all $j \neq i*$, $j = 1,2,\ldots,N$, let $q_{i*}^{\{i*,j\}} = 1$, $q_j^{\{i*,j\}} = 1 - \frac{\gamma^{i*} + \gamma^j}{(N-1)A}$. For all $j$, and $k = 1,2,\ldots,N, j \neq k \neq i*$, $q_j^{\{j,k\}} = 1 - \delta^j$, $q_k^{\{j,k\}} = 1 - \delta^k$. Let $s_m^{[m,n]\{i*,m\}} = A$, $b_{i*}^{[m,n]\{i*,m\}} = q_m^{\{i*,m\}}A$, $s_{i*}^{[m,n]\{i*,n\}} = q_m^{\{i*,m\}}A$, $b_n^{[m,n]\{i*,m\}} = q_m^{\{i*,m\}}A$.

What is happening in Example 6.2? Monetization comes from liquidity and — with scale economies — liquidity comes from trading volume. But how can monetization of trade occur where there is double coincidence of wants? The answer is scale economies. Trader $[m,n]$ wants to trade good $m$ for good $n$. He could do so directly at post $\{m,n\}$, and he would find a willing trading counterpart at the trading post, so he would only have to pay for the transaction costs on one side of the trade. But the transaction costs are still substantial, reducing his return on the trade to $A(1 - \delta^m)$ units of $n$ after starting with $A$ units of good $m$. The alternative is to trade good $m$ for good $i*$ and then trade $i*$ for $n$. This results in $A(1 - [\frac{(\gamma^{i*} + \gamma^n)}{(N-1)A}])$ units of $n$. When $N$ is sufficiently large, that is a much greater return. Because of the narrow bid−ask spread on trade through $i*$, every market with good $i*$ on one side attracts high trading volume, $N-1$ traders on each side of the market, the high trading volume needed to maintain good

Table 6.2  *Monetary equilibrium average cost pricing, bid prices – full double coincidence of wants*

| Selling:<br>Buying: | 1 | 2 | 3 | ... | $i^*$ | ... | $N-1$ | $N$ |
|---|---|---|---|---|---|---|---|---|
| 1 | X | $1-\delta^2$ | $1-\delta^3$ | : | 1 | : | $1-\delta^{N-1}$ | $1-\delta^N$ |
| 2 | $1-\delta^1$ | X | $1-\delta^3$ | : | 1 | : | $1-\delta^{N-1}$ | $1-\delta^N$ |
| 3 | $1-\delta^1$ | $1-\delta^2$ | X | : | 1 | : | $1-\delta^{N-1}$ | $1-\delta^N$ |
| ... | $1-\delta^1$ | $1-\delta^2$ | $1-\delta^3$ | X | 1 | : | $1-\delta^{N-1}$ | $1-\delta^N$ |
| $i^*$ | $1-\dfrac{\gamma^{i^*}+\gamma^1}{(N-1)A}$ | $1-\dfrac{\gamma^{i^*}+\gamma^2}{(N-1)A}$ | $1-\dfrac{\gamma^{i^*}+\gamma^3}{(N-1)A}$ | : | X | : | $1-\dfrac{\gamma^{i^*}+\gamma^{N-1}}{(N-1)A}$ | $1-\dfrac{\gamma^{i^*}+\gamma^N}{(N-1)A}$ |
| ... | $1-\delta^1$ | $1-\delta^2$ | $1-\delta^3$ | : | 1 | X | $1-\delta^{N-1}$ | $1-\delta^N$ |
| $N-1$ | $1-\delta^1$ | $1-\delta^2$ | $1-\delta^3$ | : | 1 | : | X | $1-\delta^N$ |
| $N$ | $1-\delta^1$ | $1-\delta^2$ | $1-\delta^3$ | : | 1 | : | $1-\delta^{N-1}$ | X |

$i*$'s low bid−ask spreads. The scale economy means that the choice of good $i*$ as the common medium of exchange is self-confirming.

# 3  A LARGE PURE TRADE ECONOMY WITH AVERAGE COST PRICING MONETARY EQUILIBRIUM

Since scale economies enter into this argument in an essential way, we would now like to consider a large economy. This class of examples starts with the same structure as in Example 6.2, but we allow the economy to be large in the sense that there are $\Gamma$ (positive integer) households of each type $[m, n]$. Let $\Theta^{D \times \Gamma}$ denote the $\Gamma$-fold replication of $\Theta^D$ with typical element $[m, n, g]$ where $m$ and $n$ are integers between 1 and $N$ (inclusive), $m \neq n$, and $g$ is an integer between 1 and $\Gamma$. $m$ denotes the good with which $h$ is endowed. $n$ denotes the good he prefers. $g$ is a serial number for the agent of type $[m, n]$.

**Example 6.3** (Average cost pricing monetary equilibrium in a large economy) Let the population be $\Theta^{D \times \Gamma}$. Set $r_i^{[i,j]} = A$. Let transaction technology be characterized by (TCNC). For all $1 \leq i, j \leq N$, let $\delta^i > 0$. For some $i*$ and all $j$, $1 \leq i*, j \leq N$, $i* \neq j$, let $(1 - \frac{\gamma^{i*} + \gamma^j}{\Gamma(N-1)A}) > (1 - \delta^j)$, $(1 - \frac{\gamma^{i*} + \gamma^j}{\Gamma(N-1)A}) > (1 - \delta^{i*})$. Then there is a monetary average cost pricing equilibrium with good $i*$ as the unique 'money'.

**Demonstration of Example 6.3**  The average cost large economy equilibrium pricing is shown in Table 6.3.

- For $j \neq i*, q_{i*}^{\{i*, j\}} = 1$. $q_j^{\{i*, j\}} = 1 - [(\gamma^{i*} + \gamma^j)/\Gamma A(N-1)]$.
- For all other $i, j \neq i*$, combinations, $q_i^{\{i, j\}} = (1 - \delta^j), q_j^{\{i, j\}} = (1 - \delta^j)$.
- For $h = [m, n, g]$ (where $m, n \neq i*$), we have:

$$b_n^{[m,n,g]\{i*,n\}} = Aq_m^{\{i*,m\}}$$
$$s_{i*}^{[m,n,g]\{i*,n\}} = Aq_m^{\{i*,m\}}$$
$$b_{i*}^{[m,n,g]\{i*,m\}} = Aq_m^{\{i*,m\}}$$
$$s_m^{[m,n,g]\{i*,m\}} = A.$$

- For $h = [m, n, g]$ (where $m = i*$) we have:

$$b_n^{[m, n, g]\{n, i*\}} = A.$$
$$s_{i*}^{[m, n, g]\{i, i*\}} = A.$$

Table 6.3  *Large economy monetary equilibrium average cost pricing, bid prices – full double coincidence of wants*

| Selling: | 1 | 2 | 3 | ... | $i^*$ | ... | $N-1$ | $N$ |
|---|---|---|---|---|---|---|---|---|
| **Buying:** | | | | | | | | |
| 1 | X | $1-\delta^2$ | $1-\delta^3$ | ... | 1 | ... | $1-\delta^{N-1}$ | $1-\delta^N$ |
| 2 | $1-\delta^1$ | X | $1-\delta^3$ | ... | 1 | ... | $1-\delta^{N-1}$ | $1-\delta^N$ |
| 3 | $1-\delta^1$ | $1-\delta^2$ | X | ... | 1 | ... | $1-\delta^{N-1}$ | $1-\delta^N$ |
| ... | $1-\delta^1$ | $1-\delta^2$ | $1-\delta^3$ | X | 1 | ... | $1-\delta^{N-1}$ | $1-\delta^N$ |
| $i^*$ | $1-\dfrac{\gamma^{i*}+\gamma^1}{\Gamma(N-1)A}$ | $1-\dfrac{\gamma^{i*}+\gamma^2}{\Gamma(N-1)A}$ | $1-\dfrac{\gamma^{i*}+\gamma^3}{\Gamma(N-1)A}$ | ... | X | ... | $1-\dfrac{\gamma^{i*}+\gamma^{N-1}}{\Gamma(N-1)A}$ | $1-\dfrac{\gamma^{i*}+\gamma^N}{\Gamma(N-1)A}$ |
| $N-1$ | $1-\delta^1$ | $1-\delta^2$ | $1-\delta^3$ | ... | 1 | X | X | $1-\delta^N$ |
| $N$ | $1-\delta^1$ | $1-\delta^2$ | $1-\delta^3$ | ... | 1 | ... | $1-\delta^{N-1}$ | X |

- For $h = [m, n, g]$ (where $n = i^*$), we have:

$$b_{i^*}^{[m, n, g]\{i^*, m\}} = A q_m^{\{i^*, m\}}.$$
$$s_m^{[m, n, g]\{i^*, m\}} = A.$$

The examples of this chapter demonstrate Tobin's (1959) argument: the choice of the medium of exchange is self-justifying. There is a significant resource saving in moving from a barter to a monetary equilibrium, but the choice of what is 'money' is (under these assumptions) essentially arbitrary.[2] Once the choice is made, the equilibrium, including the designation of 'money', is stable against small perturbations and entry by alternative media of exchange. These characteristics of the monetary equilibrium reflect the underlying transactions technology: the complementarity among pairwise goods markets implicit in the structure of the problem and the scale economies in transaction costs encourage concentration of trading activity in a few market-makers and a single medium of exchange.[3] Conversely, the examples of Chapter 5 suggest that scale economies are essential to unique monetization of the economy. Without assuming properties peculiar to the designated 'money' as in Example 4.1 (that 'money' is the single good so that trades that include it are achieved at the lowest possible transaction cost) there seems to be no impetus in a convex model driving the equilibrium toward a single distinguished medium of exchange. Unique monetization results from scale economies in the transaction technology.

## 4 CONCLUSION

The monetary structure of trade in general equilibrium, and the uniqueness of money in equilibrium can be demonstrated as the outcome of a market general equilibrium with scale economy in transaction costs. The existence of a unique common medium of exchange in economic equilibrium is logically derived from price theory. Starting from a (nonmonetary) Arrow–Debreu Walrasian model the addition of two constructs is sufficient: segmented markets with multiple budget constraints (one at each transaction) and scale economy in transaction costs. The multiplicity of budget constraints creates a demand for a carrier of value (medium of exchange) between transactions. Money (the common medium of exchange) arises endogenously as the most liquid (lowest transaction cost) asset. Uniqueness of the monetary instrument in equilibrium comes from scale economy in transaction costs. With sufficiently strong scale economies, monetary trade with a unique money will be adopted even in the presence of double coincidence of wants.

## NOTES

1.  This chapter is based on Starr (2003, 2004)
2.  This arbitrariness is in contrast to the example of Banerjee and Maskin (1996) where, without explicit transaction costs, in a convex model, the choice of 'money' is fully determined by the parameters of the model as the unique good whose quality is most easily recognized.
3.  The notion of scale economy is consistent with the models of Iwai (1996) and Kiyotaki and Wright (1989) where concentrating trading activity on a single transaction medium reduces waiting times for the completion of trades.

# 7. Monetization of general equilibrium[1]

In an economy with scale economies in the transaction cost function the economy converges to a monetary equilibrium with a locally unique 'money' through price-guided tâtonnement adjustment. Liquidity follows from high trading volume – so a high-volume good becomes 'money', leading to monetization of the economy's equilibrium pattern of trade.

## 1 CONVERGENCE TO A UNIQUE 'MONEY'

We learned in the previous chapter that there may be many monetary equilibria – in an economy with scale economies in the transaction cost function – each with a locally unique choice of the 'money', the locally unique common medium of exchange. How does the economy discover this equilibrium? And how does it make a choice among multiple equilibria? This chapter proposes a price-guided tâtonnement process leading to a monetary equilibrium allocation. The underlying principle is that liquidity follows from high trading volume – so if there is variation among commodities in trading volume, the high-volume goods are likely to become 'money', leading to monetization of the economy.

Einzig (1966, p. 345) suggests 'Money tends to develop automatically out of barter, through the fact that favourite means of barter are apt to arise . . . object[s] widely accepted for direct consumption'. That is, Einzig suggests that those goods with high trading volumes are the most liquid (presumably reflecting scale economy in transaction cost), and evolve into common media of exchange. That medium is unique because scale economies lead to 'money' as a natural monopoly. The following example demonstrates this process.

As monetization takes place, households supplying good $i$ and demanding good $j$ start by trading directly. They may also consider monetary trade, first trading $i$ for 'money' and then 'money' for $j$. When they discover that transaction costs are lower in this indirect trade than in direct trade of $i$ for $j$, they adopt monetary trade. Starting from a barter array consisting of $\frac{1}{2}N(N-1)$ active trading posts, the allocation evolves through price and quantity adjustments to a monetary array where only $N - 1$ trading posts are active. The impetus for the concentration of the trading function in a few trading posts (those specializing in trade that includes the commodity that is endogenously designated as 'money') in the monetary equilibrium comes from pricing the scale economies in transaction technology.

Example 7.1, below, starts with an economy of diverse endowments and demands and with a double coincidence of wants. The demand structure is arranged at the outset positing some goods most 'widely accepted for direct consumption'. With scale economies in the transaction technology, these high-volume goods will also be those with the lowest unit transaction cost. Thus they are, in Menger's view, the most saleable, and excellent candidates for '*generally* acceptable media of exchange' (1892, p. 249, original italics). As they are so adopted by some households, their trading volumes increase, reducing their average transaction costs, and making them more saleable still. This process converges to an equilibrium with a unique medium of exchange, reflecting the interaction of scale economy and liquidity. As households discover that some pairwise markets (those with high trading volumes) have lower transaction costs, they rearrange their trades to take advantage of the low cost. That leads to even higher trading volumes and even lower costs at the most active trading posts. The process converges to an equilibrium where only the high-volume trading posts dealing in a single intermediary good ('money') are in use. Under nonconvex transaction costs, this implies a cost saving, since only $N - 1$ trading posts need to operate, incurring significantly lower costs than $\frac{1}{2}N(N - 1)$ posts. Scale economies make it cost saving to concentrate transactions in a few trading posts and a unique 'money'. Scale economies in the transactions technology generate a strong tendency to multiple equilibria. This creates an interest in determining which of the several equilibria the economy will actually select. One solution to this problem is to posit an adjustment process to equilibrium that makes the choice. Hence we use the following:

**Tâtonnement adjustment process for average cost pricing equilibrium**
Prices will be adjusted by an average cost pricing auctioneer.
Specify the following adjustment process for prices:

> STEP 0: The starting point is somewhat arbitrary. In each pairwise market the bid−ask spread is set to equal average costs at low trading volume.

CYCLE 1

STEP 1: Households compute their desired trades at the posted prices and report them for each pairwise market.

STEP 2: Average costs (and average cost prices) are computed for each pairwise market based on the outcome of STEP 1. Prices are adjusted upward for goods in excess demand at a trading post, downward for goods in excess supply, with the bid−ask spread adjusted to average cost. A market's (market-making firm's) nonzero prices are specified only for those goods where the firm has the technical capability of being active in the market; other prices are unspecified, indicating no available trade; that is, trading post $\{i,j\}$ prices only goods $i,j$.

CYCLE 2 Repeat STEP 1 (at the new posted prices) and STEP 2.

CYCLE 3, CYCLE 4, . . . repeat until the process converges and trading posts clear.

## 2  A SIMPLE EXAMPLE

Einzig encourages us to look for favorite means of barter as latent money; we shall define a population with some favorite means of barter. Define a household population $\Theta^F$ as follows: let $N$ be an integer, $N \geq 3$. Without loss of generality, designate good 1 for a distinctive role: 1 is widely heavily traded. Let $\Theta^F = \{[m,n] \mid 1 \leq m,n \leq N, \ m \neq n; \ r_m^{[m,n]} = A > 0$, except $r_m^{[m,1]} = 6A = r_1^{[1,m]}$ for $m \neq 1\}$. That is, there is a distinctively high desired net trade volume in good 1(the numerical designation is inessential).

**Example 7.1** (High trading volume with scale economy designates 'money') Let the population be $\Theta^F$. Let transaction costs be characterized by (TCNC) with $\delta^i = \frac{1}{4}$, $\gamma^i = (0.6)A$, all $i$. That is, there is full double coincidence of wants. All goods have the same transaction technology but there is higher desired net trading volume in good 1. Scale economies in transaction costs are evident at trading volumes slightly higher than the desired trade size of most traders but well within the size of traders desiring net trades in good 1, particularly in exchange for 2. Then the tâtonnement process converges to a monetary equilibrium where 1 is the unique money.

**Demonstrating Example 7.1**  The economy has a full double coincidence of wants. For most pairs of goods $m,n$, the desired net trade is uniformly distributed; the desired trade between them is $A$. For pairs $1,n$ the desired trading volume is $6A$. This structure of preferences and endowments creates a desire for relatively high trading volumes among households trading in good 1.

The scale economy in transactions costs begins to be apparent at trading volumes just slightly larger than the endowment of most households. The scale economy is manifest well within the desired trading volumes of households endowed with or desiring good 1. The progression from barter to money is then the movement from a diffuse array of many active low-volume markets to the concentration on a connected family of high-volume (low average cost) markets. The tâtonnement proceeds as follows:

STEP 0: For all $1 \leq i, j \leq N$, $i \neq j$, $q_i^{\{i,j\}} = q_j^{\{i,j\}} = \frac{3}{4}$.
CYCLE 1, STEP 1:

- For $[m,n] \in \Theta^F, m \neq 1 \neq n, b_n^{[m,n]\{m,n\}} = (\frac{3}{4})A = q_m^{\{m,n\}}A, s_m^{[m,n]\{m,n\}} = A$; all other purchases and sales are nil.
- For $[m, 1] \in \Theta^F$, $b_1^{[m,n]\{m,n\}} = (4.5)A = q_m^{\{m,1\}}6A$, $s_m^{[m,n]\{m,1\}} = 6A$; all other purchases and sales are nil. For $[1, n] \in \Theta^F$, $b_n^{[1,n]\{1,n\}} = (4.5)A = q_1^{\{1,n\}}6A$, $s_1^{[1,n]\{1,n\}} = 6A$; all other purchases and sales are nil.

STEP 2:

- For $\{m,n\}$ where $m \neq 1 \neq n$, $q_m^{\{m,n\}} = q_n^{\{m,n\}} = (\frac{3}{4})$.
- For $\{m,1\}$, $\{1,m\}$, $q_m^{\{m,1\}} = q_1^{\{m,1\}} = \frac{6A - \gamma}{6A} = 0.90$.

At this stage we can see the initial effect of the scale economy. At STEP 0 prices started essentially equivalent in all pairwise markets. But the prices announced at the end of CYCLE 1 STEP 2 show that the bid prices of goods are much higher in the highest volume markets; the bid−ask spread is lower there. The high-volume market is more liquid.

On entering CYCLE 2 STEP 1 households recalculate their desired trades. Those who have been trading on $\{m, 1\}$ find that trade on these markets has become even more attractive since the bid−ask spreads have narrowed. Those who had been trading on $\{m,n\}$ face a quandary: goods $m$, $n$ are the goods that they want to trade, but trading indirectly through good 1 in $\{n,1\}$ and $\{m, 1\}$ may be a lower-cost alternative. In order to make that decision the household compares $q_m^{\{n,m\}}$ to the product $q_1^{\{m,1\}} \cdot q_m^{\{m,1\}}$. The former is the value of $m$ in terms of $n$ in direct trade, the latter through trade mediated by good 1. $q_m^{\{m,1\}} \cdot q_1^{\{2,1\}} = 0.9 \times 0.9 = 0.81 > 0.75 = q_m^{\{m,n\}}$. Household $[m,n]$ can get more $n$ for its $m$ by trading indirectly through the markets with good 1, and household $[n, m]$ can get more $m$ for its $n$ by trading indirectly through the markets with good 1. They decide to trade through good 1. Good 1 has taken on the character of money.

CYCLE 2, STEP 1:

- For $[m,n] \in \Theta^F$, $m,n \neq 1$, $s_m^{[m,n]\{1,m\}} = A$, $b_1^{[m,n]\{1,m\}} = 0.9A$, $s_1^{[m,n]\{1,n\}} = 0.9A$, $b_n^{[m,n]\{1,n\}} = 0.81A$, all other purchases and sales are nil.
- For $[m,1]$, $[1,m]$, $s_m^{[m,1]\{m,1\}} = 6A$,
- $b_1^{[m,1]\{m,1\}} = 6Aq_m^{\{m,1\}} = 5.4A$; all other purchases and sales are nil. For $[1,n]$, $s_1^{[1,n]\{1,n\}} = 6A$, $b_n^{[1,n]\{1,n\}} = 6Aq_1^{\{n,1\}} = 5.4A$; all other purchases and sales are nil.

As CYCLE 2 STEP 1 is completed, trade has become fully monetized. CONVERGENCE.

What is happening in Example 7.1? Preferences and endowments are structured so that at roughly the same prices for all goods, there is a balance between supply and demand. Some pairs of goods are more actively traded than others. Good 1 has approximately six times as much active demand (and supply) as most other goods.

Here is how trade takes place. The starting point is a barter economy, the full array of $\frac{1}{2}N(N-1)$ trading posts. For every pair of goods $i, j$, where $1 \leq i, j \leq N$, there is a post where that pair can be traded. The starting prices are chosen (somewhat arbitrarily) to cover average costs at low trading volume. The bid−ask spread is uniform across trading posts so trade at each post is as attractive as anywhere else. Then each household computes its demands and supplies at those prices. It figures out what it wants to buy and sell and to which trading posts it should go to implement the trades. Since all bid−ask spreads start out equal, each household just goes to the post that trades in the pair of goods that the household wants to exchange; demanders of good $j$ who are endowed with good $i$ go to $\{i, j\}$. Because of the distribution of demands and supplies, there is six times the trading volume on posts $\{1, j\}$ as on most $\{i, j\}$.

Then the average cost pricing auctioneer responds to the planned transactions. He prices bid−ask spreads in all markets to cover the costs of the trade on them. Since there is a scale economy in the transactions technology, this leads to narrower bid−ask spreads on the $\{1, j\}$. The auctioneer announces his prices.

Households respond to the new prices. The market makers on the many different $\{i, 1\}$ markets find their trading volumes increased. Trade is fully monetized with good 1 as the 'money'.

The average cost pricing auctioneer reprices the markets. Inactive markets, $\{i, j\}$ for $i \neq 1 \neq j$, necessarily continue to post their starting prices (which reflected anticipated low trading volume). The active markets $\{i, 1\}$ get posted prices reflecting their high trading volumes, with narrow bid−ask spreads.

Households review the newly posted prices. The narrow bid−ask spreads on the $\{i, 1\}$ markets reinforce the attractiveness of their previous plans, which called for trading through good 1 as an intermediary. They leave their monetary trading plans in force. At current prices, it is much more economical to trade $i$ for $j$ by first trading $i$ for 1 and then 1 for $j$ than to trade $i$ for $j$ directly. High trading volumes on the $\{i, 1\}$ and $\{j, 1\}$ markets ensure low transaction costs and keep them attractive. All trade takes place at $\{i, 1\}$, $i = 2, 3, 4, \ldots, N$. Good 1 has become the unique 'money'.

Example 7.1 demonstrates price and trading adjustment to the property that scale economies in the transactions technology mean that high-volume markets will be low-average cost markets. The transition from barter to monetary exchange is the transition from a complex of many thin markets − one for trade of each pair of goods for one another − to an array of a smaller number of thick markets dealing in each good versus a unique common medium of exchange. This transition is resource saving when scale economies in transactions technology are large enough.

## 3  MONETIZATION WITH ABSENCE OF DOUBLE COINCIDENCE OF WANTS

The previous examples have focused on tâtonnement monetization with double coincidence of wants. That approach is particularly convenient to model because of the immediate equation of supply and demand at each trading post. The remarkable result there is that despite the double coincidence of wants, monetary equilibrium exists and is the limit of the tâtonnement adjustment. This is distinctive inasmuch as the *absence* of double coincidence of wants has long been emphasized as the reason for the usefulness of money. In the examples above, the driving force was not absence of double coincidence of wants, but rather scale economies in transaction cost leading to a corner solution. The corner solution is zero activity in most trading posts and high level of activity in the small number of active trading posts.

Now it is time to investigate the classic issue of absence of double coincidence of wants. Will the same sort of tâtonnement convergence take place there? We shall start with an example designed to parallel those of Chapters 4 and 6 with enough asymmetry − emphasis on a single commodity trade to create a scale economy early in the tâtonnement process.

The population of trading households is modified from Chapter 4 including two subpopulations denoted $\Theta$ (similar to $\Theta$ in Chapter 4) and $\Psi$.

Consider a pure exchange trading post economy with $N$ commodities, $N \geq 5$. $\Omega$ denotes the greatest integer $\leq (N - 1)/2$.

Let $[i, j]$ denote a household endowed with good $i$ that prefers good $j$; $i \neq j, i, j = 1, 2, \ldots, N$. Denote the endowment of $[i, j]$ as $r_i^{[i,j]}$. $[i, j]$'s utility function is $u^{[i,j]}(x_1, x_2, x_3, \ldots, x_N) = x_j$. That is, household $[i, j]$ values good $j$ only. It cares for $i$ only as a resource to trade for $j$. This is obviously an immense oversimplification — but it serves to focus the issue.

Einzig encourages us to look for favorite means of barter as latent money; we shall define a population with some favorite means of barter. Define a household subpopulation $\Psi$ as follows: let $N$ be an integer, $N \geq 5$. Without loss of generality, designate good 1 for a distinctive role: 1 is widely heavily traded. Let $\Psi = \{ [m, 1], [1, m] \mid 1 < m \leq N;$ $r_m^{[m,1]} = 4A = r_1^{[1,m]} \}$. That is, there is a distinctively high desired net trade volume in good 1 (the numerical designation is inessential) and within $\Psi$ there is a double coincidence of wants.

Consider a subpopulation denoted $\Theta$ of households including $\Omega$ households endowed with each good and each household desiring a good different from its endowment. There are $\Omega$ households endowed with good 1, preferring respectively, goods 2, 3, 4, ..., $\Omega + 1$: $[1, 2], [1, 3], [1, 4]$, ..., $[1, \Omega + 1]$. There are $\Omega$ households endowed with good 2, preferring respectively, goods 3, 4, 5, ..., $\Omega + 2$: $[2, 3], [2, 4], [2, 5], \ldots, [2, \Omega + 2]$. The roll call of households proceeds through $[N, 1], [N, 2], [N, 3], \ldots, [N, \Omega]$. $r_i^{[i,j]} = A$.

As before, we can envisage $\Theta$'s elements $[i, j]$ set round a clock-face at a position corresponding to the endowed good, $i$, eager to acquire $j$. $j$ being $1, 2, \ldots, \Omega$, steps clockwise from $i$. Population $\Theta$ displays absence of double coincidence of wants. For each household endowed with good $i$ and desiring good $j$, $[i, j]$, there is no precise mirror image, $[j, i]$. Nevertheless, there are $\Omega$ households endowed with one unit of commodity $i$, and $\Omega$ households strongly preferring commodity $i$ to all others. That is true for each good. Thus gross supplies equal gross demands, though there is no immediate opportunity for any two households to make a mutually advantageous trade. Jevons (1875) tells us that this is precisely the setting where money is suitable to facilitate trade. One way to visualize $\Theta$'s situation is to think of the households arrayed in a circle clockwise, each one's position designated by endowment. They can arrange a Pareto-improving redistribution by each taking its endowment and sending it $|i - j|$ places counterclockwise. However, reflecting the absence of double coincidence of wants, if each of the households in $\Theta$ goes to the trading post where its endowment is traded against its desired good, it finds itself alone. It is dealing on a thin market. The following Example 7.2 demonstrates that, with scale economies in transaction cost, the high-volume good becomes money, just as Einzig posits.

**Example 7.2** (High trading volume with scale economy designates 'money') Let the population be $\Theta \cup \Psi$. Let transactions costs be characterized by (TCNC) with $\delta^i = \frac{1}{4}$, $\gamma^i = (0.6)A$, all $i$. Since these values are common, we shall omit the superscripts, using as notation only $\delta, \gamma$. That is, there is absence of double coincidence of wants, except for the high-volume households in $\Psi$. All goods have the same transaction technology but there is higher desired net trading volume in good 1. Scale economies in transaction costs are evident at trading volumes higher than the desired trade size of most traders but well within the size of traders desiring net trades in good 1. Then the tâtonnement process converges to a monetary equilibrium where 1 is the unique money.

**Demonstrating Example 7.2:**   The subpopulation $\Psi$ has full double coincidence of wants. For $[1, j]$ and $[j, 1]$ in $\Psi$ the desired trading volume is $4A$. This structure of preferences and endowments creates a desire for relatively high trading volumes among households trading in good 1.

The scale economy in transaction costs begins to be apparent at trading volumes significantly larger than the endowment of households in $\Theta$. The scale economy shows up first in the trading pricing of trades undertaken in good 1, by households in $\Psi$. The progression from barter to money is then the movement from a diffuse array of many active low-volume markets to the concentration on a connected family of high-volume (low-average cost) markets. The tâtonnement proceeds as follows:

STEP 0: For all $1 \leq i, j \leq N$, $i \neq j$, $q_i^{\{i,j\}} = q_j^{\{i,j\}} = 1 - \frac{1}{4} = 0.75$.
CYCLE 1, STEP 1:

- For $[m, n] \in \Theta, m \neq n, b_n^{[m,n]\{m,n\}} = (\frac{3}{4})A = q_m^{\{m,n\}}A, s_m^{[m,n]\{m,n\}} = A$; all other purchases and sales are nil.
- For $[m, 1] \in \Psi$, $b_1^{[m,n]\{m,n\}} = 3A = q_m^{\{m,1\}}4A$, $s_m^{[m,n]\{m,1\}} = 4A$; all other purchases and sales are nil. For $[1, n] \in \Psi$, $b_n^{[1,n]\{1,n\}} = 3A = q_1^{\{1,n\}}4A$, $s_1^{[1,n]\{1,n\}} = 4A$; all other purchases and sales are nil.

STEP 2:

- For $\{m, n\}$ where $m \neq 1 \neq n$, $q_m^{\{m,n\}} = q_n^{\{m,n\}} = (1 - \delta)^2 = (\frac{3}{4})^2 = (0.75)^2 = 0.56$.
- For $\{m, 1\}$, $q_m^{\{m,1\}} = q_1^{\{m,1\}} = \max[\frac{4A - \gamma}{4A}, \frac{3}{4}] = 0.85$.

At this stage we can see the initial effect of the scale economy. At STEP 0 prices started essentially equivalent in all pairwise markets. But the prices announced at the end of CYCLE 1 STEP 2 show that the bid prices of goods are much higher in the high-volume markets; the bid−ask spread is lower there. The high-volume markets are more liquid. And the low-volume markets are very illiquid; it turned out that at typical $\{i, j\}, i, j \neq 1$ there was only one side of supply or demand present − meaning that both transaction costs on the buy side and sell side had to be absorbed there.

On entering CYCLE 2 STEP 1, households recalculate their desired trades. Those who have been trading on $\{m, 1\}$ find that trade on these markets has become even more attractive since the bid−ask spreads have narrowed. Those who had been trading on $\{i, j\}, i, j \neq 1$ face a quandary: goods $i$ and $j$ are the goods that they want to trade, but trading indirectly through good 1 $\{j, 1\}$ and $\{i, 1\}$ may be a lower cost alternative. Household $[i, j], i, j \neq 1$ compares $q_j^{\{i,j\}} = 0.56$ to the product $q_i^{\{i,1\}} \cdot q_1^{\{j,1\}}$. The former is the value of $i$ in terms of $j$ in direct trade, the latter through trade mediated by good 1. $q_i^{\{i,1\}} \cdot q_1^{\{j,1\}} = (0.85)^2 = 0.72 > 0.56 = q_i^{\{i,j\}}$. Household $[i, j]$ can get more $j$ for its $i$ by trading indirectly through the markets with good 1. It decides to trade through good 1. Good 1 has taken on the character of money.

CYCLE 2, STEP 1:

- For $[1, j], [i, 1] \in \Psi$, $i, j \neq 1$, $s_1^{[1,j]\{1,j\}} = 4A$, $b_j^{[1,j]\{1,j\}} = 4Aq_1^{\{1,j\}}$; $s_i^{[i,1]\{i,1\}} = 4A$, $b_1^{[i,1]\{i,1\}} = 4Aq_1^{\{i,1\}}$; all other purchases and sales are nil.

- For $[i, j] \in \Theta$, $i \neq 1 \neq j$, $s_i^{[i,j]\{i,1\}} = A$, $b_1^{[i,j]\{i,1\}} = 4Aq_i^{\{i,1\}}$, $s_1^{[i,j]\{1,j\}} = 4Aq_i^{\{i,1\}}$, $b_j^{[i,j]\{1,j\}} = 4Aq_i^{\{i,1\}}q_1^{\{1,j\}}$; all other purchases and sales are nil.

STEP 2:

- For $\{m, n\}$ where $m \neq 1 \neq n$, $q_m^{\{m,n\}} = q_n^{\{m,n\}} = (1 - \delta)^2 = (\frac{3}{4})^2 = (0.75)^2 = 0.56$.
- For $\{m, 1\}$, $q_m^{\{m,1\}} = 1$, $q_1^{\{m,1\}} = \frac{(4 + \Omega)A - \gamma}{(4 + \Omega)A} \geq 0.914$.

As CYCLE 2 STEP 1 is completed, trade has become fully monetized. All trade goes through good 1 as a medium of exchange. As STEP 2 is completed, prices reflect the higher trading volumes on markets including 1.

CYCLE 3, STEP 1: Repeat Cycle 2, Step 1.
STEP 2: Repeat Cycle 2, Step 2.
CONVERGENCE.

What is happening in Example 7.2? Some pairs of goods are more actively traded than others. Good 1 has approximately four times as much active demand (and supply) as most other goods.

Here is how trade takes place. The starting point is a barter economy, the full array of $\frac{1}{2}N(N-1)$ trading posts. For every pair of goods $i, j$, where $1 \leq i, j \leq N$, there is a post where that pair can be traded. The starting prices are chosen (somewhat arbitrarily) to cover average costs at low trading volume. The bid−ask spread is uniform across trading posts so trade at each post is as attractive as anywhere else. Then each household computes its demands and supplies at those prices. It figures out what it wants to buy and sell and to which trading posts it should go to implement the trades. Since all bid−ask spreads start out equal, each household just goes to the post that trades in the pair of goods that the household wants to exchange; demanders of good $j$ who are endowed with good $i$ go to $\{i, j\}$. Because of the distribution of demands and supplies, there is eight times the trading volume on posts $\{1, j\}$ as on most $\{i, j\}$.

Then the average cost pricing auctioneer responds to the planned transactions. He prices bid−ask spreads in all markets to cover the costs of the trade on them. Since there is a scale economy in the transactions technology, this leads to narrower bid−ask spreads on the $\{1, j\}$ trading posts. The auctioneer announces his prices.

Households respond to the new prices. Households who want to buy or sell good $i$ discover that the bid−ask spread on market $\{1, i\}$ is lower than on any other market trading $i$. It makes sense to channel transactions through this low cost market, even if the household has to undertake additional transactions to do so. Ordinarily households $[i, j]$ and $[j, i]$ would have gone directly to the market $\{i, j\}$ to do their trading. But the combined transaction costs on $\{i, 1\}$ and on $\{1, j\}$ are lower than those on $\{i, j\}$. Households $[i, j]$ and $[j, i]$ find that they incur lower transaction costs by trading through good 1 as an intermediary. They exchange $i$ for 1 and 1 for $j$ (or $j$ for 1 and 1 for $i$) rather than trade directly. The market makers on the many different $\{i, 1\}$ markets, $2 \leq i \leq N$, find their trading volumes increase as the $[i, j]$ and $[j, i]$ traders move their trades to $\{i, 1\}$ and $\{j, 1\}$.

The average cost pricing auctioneer responds to the revised trading plans once again. Bid−ask spreads narrow on $\{i, 1\}$, $2 \leq i \leq N$. Now the discounts incurred through bid−ask spreads in trading for $i \neq 1 \neq j$ indirectly − through $\{i, 1\}$ and $\{1, j\}$ − are significantly smaller than those trading directly at $\{i,j\}$ (particularly when $N$ is large). The auctioneer announces his prices. Households respond to the new prices. For all households $[i,j]$, it is now less expensive to trade through good 1 as an intermediary than to trade directly $i$ for $j$ or $j$ for $i$. All $[i,j]$ now trade on $\{i, 1\}$ and $\{j, 1\}$; none trade on $\{i,j\}$, for $i \neq 1 \neq j$. Trade is fully monetized with good 1 as the 'money'.

The average cost pricing auctioneer reprices the markets. Inactive markets, $\{i,j\}$ for $i \neq 1 \neq j$, continue to post their low- or zero-volume prices (which reflect anticipated low trading volume). The active markets $\{i, 1\}$ get posted prices reflecting their high trading volumes, with narrow bid−ask spreads.

Households review the newly posted prices. The narrow bid−ask spreads on the $\{i, 1\}$ markets reinforce the attractiveness of their previous plans, which called for trading through good 1 as an intermediary. They leave their monetary trading plans in force. At current prices, it is much more economical to trade $i$ for $j$ by first trading $i$ for 1 and then 1 for $j$ than to trade $i$ for $j$ directly. High trading volumes on the $\{i, 1\}$ and $\{j, 1\}$ markets ensure low transaction costs and keep them attractive. All trade takes place at $\{i, 1\}$, $i = 2, 3, 4, \ldots, N$. Good 1 has become the unique 'money'.

Example 7.2 demonstrates price and trading adjustment to the property that scale economies in the transactions technology mean that high-volume markets will be low average cost markets. It does so in the classical context of absence of double coincidence of wants. The transition from barter to monetary exchange is the transition from a complex of many thin markets − one for trade of each pair of goods for one another − to an array of a smaller number of thick markets dealing in each good versus a unique common medium of exchange. This transition is resource saving when scale economies in transactions technology are large enough.

# 4  LEARNING TO TRADE MONETARILY

Examples 7.1 and 7.2 demonstrate the transition to monetary trade. Trading patterns progress through individually rational decisions when prices reflect the scale economy and the initial condition includes a commodity (the latent 'money') with a relatively high transaction volume (hence low average transaction cost). Then, as Einzig notes, 'favourite means of barter are apt to arise' and a barter economy thus converges incrementally to a monetary economy. Menger (1892, p. 248) describes this transition:

> [W]hen any one has brought goods not highly saleable to market, the idea uppermost in his mind is to exchange them, not only for such as he happens to be in need of, but . . . for other goods . . . more saleable than his own . . . By . . . a mediate exchange, he gains the prospect of accomplishing his purpose more surely and economically than if he had confined himself to direct exchange . . . Men have been led . . . without convention, without legal compulsion . . . to exchange . . . their wares . . . for other goods . . . more saleable . . . which . . . have . . . become generally acceptable media of exchange.

Thus, Menger argues that starting from a relatively primitive market setting, some goods will be more liquid than others. As they are adopted as media of exchange, markets for trade in them versus other goods become increasingly liquid. Eventually they become the common media of exchange in equilibrium. Examples 7.1 and 7.2 formalize this argument emphasizing that the increasing liquidity develops endogenously as a result of scale economy in the transaction process.

## NOTE

1.  This chapter is based on Starr (2003, 2004).

# 8.   Government-issued fiat money[1]

One of the observations this book began with was that money is almost universally uniquely government-issued fiat money (and instruments denominated and convertible thereto) trading at a positive price though it produces no output or utility. There are two issues here: why the positive price, why the universal usage? Positive price comes from acceptability in payment in taxes (a notion that goes back to Adam Smith). Universal usage comes from the scale economy noted in Chapter 6 and government's large scale, leading the economy to a corner solution where government money is the natural monopoly medium of exchange.

## 1   TAXATION AND MONEY

In order to study fiat money we introduce a government with the unique power to issue fiat money. Fiat money is intrinsically worthless; it enters no one's utility function. But government is uniquely capable of declaring it acceptable in payment of taxes. Adam Smith (1776) notes 'A prince, who should enact that a certain proportion of his taxes be paid in a paper money of a certain kind, might thereby give a certain value to this paper money' (Vol. I, Book II, ch. 2, p. 398). Abba Lerner (1947, p. 313) comments,

> The modern state can make anything it chooses generally acceptable as money and thus establish its value quite apart from any connection, even of the most formal kind, with gold or with backing of any kind. It is true that a simple declaration that such and such is money will not do, even if backed by the most convincing constitutional evidence of the state's absolute sovereignty. But if the state is willing to accept the proposed money in payment of taxes and other obligations to itself the trick is done . . . On the other hand if the state should decline to accept some kind of money in payment of obligations to itself, it is difficult to believe that it would retain much of its general acceptability.

Taxation − and fiat money's guaranteed value in payment of taxes − explains the positive equilibrium value of fiat money.[2] That fiat money is legal tender is essentially meaningless without a guarantee of the price at which it may be tendered. But acceptability in payment of taxes at a fixed rate creates a market-based value. Government's large scale along with scale economies in transaction costs — as in Chapter 6 — explain fiat money's uniqueness as the medium of exchange.

As an economic agent, government is denoted $G$. Government sells tax receipts, the $N + 1$th good. It also sells good $N + 2$, an intrinsically worthless instrument, (latent) fiat money, that government undertakes to accept in payment of taxes, that is, in exchange for $N + 1$.

Recall the population of households $\Theta$ from Chapter 4. Set $r_i^{[i,j]} = A$. We modify $\Theta$ very slightly to take account of taxes, denoting it $\Theta^T$. Recall that $\Omega$ denotes the greatest integer $\leq (N - 1)/2$, and for each good there are $\Omega$ households endowed therewith, each desiring a different good. There is complete absence of double coincidence of wants.

The typical household $[i, j]$ in $\Theta^T$ desires to purchase tax receipts to the extent it prefers not to have a quarrel with the government's tax authorities. Government sets a target tax receipt purchase by the taxpayer of $\tau^{[i,j]}$. Then we rewrite $[i, j]$'s utility function as:

$$u^{[i,j]}(x) = x_j - 2\{\max[(\tau^{[i,j]} - x_{N+1}^{[i,j]}), 0]\} \quad (UT) \qquad (8.1)$$

That is, household $[i, j]$ values paying its taxes with a positive marginal utility up to its tax bill $\tau^{[i,j]}$ and with zero marginal utility for tax payments thereafter. Government uses its revenue to purchase a variety of goods $n = 1, \ldots, N$, in the amount $x_n^G$.

Good $N + 2$ good represents latent fiat money. Government, $G$, sells $N + 1$ (tax receipts) for $N + 2$ at a fixed ratio of one for one. The trading post $\{N + 1, N + 2\}$ where tax receipts are traded for $N + 2$ operates with zero transaction cost. Acceptability in payment of taxes ensures $N + 2$'s positive value. If, in addition, $N + 2$ is assumed to have sufficiently low transaction cost, then it becomes the common medium of exchange. This result represents the adaptation of Example 5.1 to the setting with fiat money and taxation.

For the model with taxation, define the linear transaction cost in the following way, as in Chapter 4:

**Definition**   T-system transaction cost
   $C^{\{i,j\}} = \delta \times$ (volume of goods $i$ and $j$ purchased by the post)
   Marginal cost of trading $i$ for $j$ is $\delta$ times the gross quantity traded.
   Trading good $N + 2$ is assumed to be costless. Thus,
   $C^{\{N+2,j\}} = \delta \times$ (volume of good $j$ purchased by the post), for $j = 1, 2, \ldots, N$.
   Finally, the tax payment is assumed to be have zero transaction cost:

$$C^{\{N+1,N+2\}} = 0.$$

**Proposition 8.1** Let the population of households be $\Theta^T$. Let $u^{[i,j]}$ be described by (UT). Let $\tau^0 > 0$ be a constant. Let $0 < \tau^{[i,j]} = \tau^0 < A(1 - \delta^{N+2})(1 - \delta^i)$, all $[i,j] \in \Theta^T$. Let $x_n^G = \Omega\tau^0 q_{N+2}^{\{N+2,n\}}$ all $n = 1, 2, \ldots, N$. Let $C^{\{i,j\}}$ be the T-system transaction cost. Then the unique average cost (and marginal cost) pricing equilibrium is a monetary equilibrium with good $N + 2$ as the common medium of exchange.

**Demonstration of Proposition** $q_{N+2}^{\{N+1,N+2\}} = 1.$ $q_j^{\{N+2,j\}} = 1 - \delta$, for all $j = 1, 2, \ldots, N.$ $q_{N+2}^{\{N+2,j\}} = 1$, for all $j = 1, 2, \ldots, N.$ $q_j^{\{i,j\}} = (1 - \delta)^2$, for all $i \neq j, i, j = 1, 2, \ldots, N.$ Hence, all trade in $j = 1, 2, \ldots, N$ goes through trading posts $\{j, N + 2\}$ as the low-cost venue.

**Definition** TCNC-T, scale economy transaction cost with taxation
The nonconvex (scale economy) cost function[3] for trading post $\{i, j\}$, $i, j = 1, 2, \ldots, N, N + 2$ is:

$$C^{\{i,j\}} = \min[\delta^i y_i^{\{i,j\}B}, \gamma^i] + \min[\delta^j y_j^{\{i,j\}B}, \gamma^j] \qquad \text{(TCNC-T)}$$
$$C^{\{N+1,j\}} \gg 2\gamma^j, \text{ for } j = 1, 2, \ldots, N, \text{ and}$$
$$C^{\{N+1,N+2\}} = 0,$$

where $\delta^i, \delta^j, \gamma^i, \gamma^j > 0$. In words, the transaction technology looks like this: trading post $\{i, j\}$ makes a market in goods $i$ and $j$, buying each good in order to resell it. Transaction costs vary directly (in proportions $\delta^i, \delta^j$) with volume of trade at low volume and then hit a ceiling, after which they do not increase with trading volume. Just as in Chapters 6 and 7, the specification in (TCNC-T) is an extreme case: zero marginal transaction cost beyond the ceiling. Trading $N + 2$ for $N + 1$ is transaction costless. Trading other goods for $N + 1$ (trying to pay your taxes in kind, rather than in fiat money) has a high transaction cost.

**Proposition 8.2** Let the population of households be $\Theta^T$. Let $u^{[i,j]}$ be described by (UT). Let $\tau^0 > 0$ be a constant. Let $0 < \tau^{[i,j]} = \tau^0 < A(1 - \delta^{N+2})(1 - \delta^i)$, all $[i,j] \in \Theta^T$. Let $x_n^G = \Omega\tau^0 q_{N+2}^{\{N+2,n\}}$ and $\Omega\tau^0 > \gamma^n/\delta^n$ all $n = 1, 2, \ldots, N, N + 2$. Let $C^{\{i,j\}}$ be (TCNC-T). Then there is an average cost pricing monetary equilibrium with good $N + 2$ as the unique common medium of exchange.

**Demonstration of Proposition 8.2** For $n, m \neq N + 2$, set $q_n^{\{m,n\}} = (1 - \delta^n)(1 - \delta^m).$ $q_n^{\{N+2,n\}} = 1, q_{N+2}^{\{N+2,n\}} = (1 - \frac{\gamma^n}{\Omega A})(1 - \frac{\gamma^{N+2}}{\Omega A})$ (see Table 8.1). Then all trade in $i = 1, 2, \ldots, N$ goes through trading posts $\{i, N + 2\}$ as the low-cost venue.

*Table 8.1  Government-issued monetary equilibrium average cost pricing, bid prices*

| Selling: | 1 | 2 | 3 | ⋯ | N | ⋯ | N+1 | N+2 |
|---|---|---|---|---|---|---|---|---|
| Buying: 1 | X | $(1-\delta^1)(1-\delta^2)$ | $(1-\delta^1)(1-\delta^3)$ | ⋯ | $(1-\delta^1)(1-\delta^N)$ | ⋯ | $(1-\delta^1)(1-\delta^{N+1})$ | $(1-\frac{\gamma^1}{\Omega A})(1-\frac{\gamma^{N+2}}{\Omega A})$ |
| 2 | $(1-\delta^1)(1-\delta^2)$ | X | $(1-\delta^3)(1-\delta^2)$ | ⋯ | $(1-\delta^2)(1-\delta^N)$ | ⋯ | $(1-\delta^2)(1-\delta^{N+1})$ | $(1-\frac{\gamma^2}{\Omega A})(1-\frac{\gamma^{N+2}}{\Omega A})$ |
| 3 | $(1-\delta^3)(1-\delta^1)$ | $(1-\delta^3)(1-\delta^2)$ | X | ⋯ | $(1-\delta^3)(1-\delta^N)$ | ⋯ | $(1-\delta^3)(1-\delta^{N+1})$ | $(1-\frac{\gamma^3}{\Omega A})(1-\frac{\gamma^{N+2}}{\Omega A})$ |
| ⋮ | ⋮ | ⋮ | ⋮ | X | ⋮ | | ⋮ | ⋮ |
| N | $(1-\delta^1)(1-\delta^N)$ | $(1-\delta^2)(1-\delta^N)$ | $(1-\delta^3)(1-\delta^N)$ | ⋯ | X | ⋯ | $(1-\delta^N)(1-\delta^{N+1})$ | $(1-\frac{\gamma^N}{\Omega A})(1-\frac{\gamma^{N+2}}{\Omega A})$ |
| N+1 | $(1-\delta^1)(1-\delta^{N+1})$ | $(1-\delta^2)(1-\delta^{N+1})$ | $(1-\delta^3)(1-\delta^{N+1})$ | ⋯ | $(1-\delta^N)(1-\delta^{N+1})$ | ⋯ | X | 1 |
| N+2 | 1 | 1 | 1 | ⋯ | 1 | ⋯ | 1 | X |

As is common in the setting of scale economy, there are multiple equilibria. Though $N + 2$ could be the monetary instrument (as suggested in Proposition 8.2 above) that is not guaranteed. Any commonly traded good, with trading volume sufficiently high to activate the scale economy, could become the common medium of exchange. Why should $N + 2$ become money? If government is a large economic agent, active at high volume in many goods markets, then government-issued $N + 2$ is a high-volume instrument, generating scale economies in transaction costs. Then in a dynamic adjustment, the economy will approach an allocation where $N + 2$ is the common medium of exchange. Suppose the same tâtonnement adjustment process for average cost pricing equilibrium as in Chapter 7. That plausible adjustment process explains why government-issued fiat money becomes the unique common medium of exchange – and would do so even in the absence of legal tender rules. Government has two distinctive characteristics: it has the power to support the value of fiat money by making it acceptable in payment of taxes; it is a large economic presence undertaking a high volume of transactions in the economy. Hence, government can make its fiat money the common medium of exchange merely by using it as such. The scale economies implied will make fiat money the low transaction cost instrument and hence the most suitable medium of exchange, not just for government but for all transactors.

**Proposition 8.3** Let the population of households be $\Theta^T$. Let $u^{[i,j]}$ be described by (UT). Let $\tau^0 > 0$ be a constant. Let $0 < \tau^{[i,j]} = \tau^0 < A(1 - \delta^{N+2})(1 - \delta^i)$, all $[i,j] \in \Theta^T$. Let $x_n^G = \Omega\tau^0 q_{N+2}^{\{N+2,n\}}$ all $n = 1, 2, \ldots, N$. Let $C^{[i,j]}$ be described by (TCNC-T). Let $(\gamma^{N+2}/\Omega\tau^0) < \delta^i$ all $i = 1, 2, \ldots, N$. Then there exists a monetary average cost pricing equilibrium with taxation with good $N + 2$ as the unique 'money'. That monetary equilibrium is the unique limit point of the tâtonnement adjustment.

**Demonstration of Proposition 8.3** The notation $n \oplus j$ denotes $n + j$ mod $N$. Existence of the monetary equilibrium is demonstrated in Proposition 8.2 above. Convergence is argued below:

STEP 0: For $n \neq m$ set $q_n^{\{m,n\}} = (1 - \delta^n)$.
CYCLE 1, STEP 1:

- For $\ell = 1, 2, \ldots, \Omega$, let $s_n^{[n, n\oplus\ell]\{n, n\oplus\ell\}} = A - (\tau^0/q_n^{\{N+2,n\}})$, $b_{n\oplus\ell}^{[n, n\oplus\ell]\{n, n\oplus\ell\}} = (A - (\tau^0/q_n^{\{N+2,n\}}))q_n^{\{n, n\oplus\ell\}}$, $s_{N+2}^{[n, n\oplus\ell]\{N+2, N+1\}} = \tau^0 = b_{N+1}^{[n, n\oplus\ell]\{N+2,n\}}$; $b_{N+2}^{[n, n\oplus\ell]\{N+2,n\}} = \tau^0$, $s_n^{[n, n\oplus\ell]\{N+2,n\}} = \tau^0/q_n^{\{N+2,n\}}$.

- For $n = 1, 2, \ldots, N$, let $s_{N+2}^{G\{N+2,n\}} = \Omega\tau^0$, $b_n^{G\{N+2,n\}} = \Omega\tau^0 q_{N+2}^{\{N+2,n\}}$.

CYCLE 1, STEP 2:

- For $n, m \neq N + 2$, $n \neq m$, set $q_n^{\{m,n\}} = (1 - \delta^n)$. $\min[\delta^n, \gamma^n/\Omega\tau^0] = \gamma^n/\Omega\tau^0$. Thus $q_n^{\{N+2,n\}} = (1 - \gamma^n/\Omega\tau^0)$ $(1 - \gamma^{N+2}/\Omega\tau^0)$, $q_{N+2}^{\{N+2,n\}} = 1$.

CYCLE 2, STEP 1:

- For $n = 1, 2, \ldots, N$, let $s_{N+2}^{G\{N+2,n\}} = \Omega\tau^0$, $b_n^{G\{N+2,n\}} = \Omega\tau^0 q_{N+2}^{\{N+2,n\}}$; $s_{N+1}^{G\{N+1,N+2\}} = N\Omega\tau^0$, $b_{N+2}^{G\{N+1,N+2\}} = N\Omega\tau^0$; $b_{N+1}^{[n,n\oplus\ell]\{N+2,N+1\}} = \tau^0$, $s_{N+2}^{[n,n\oplus\ell]\{N+2,N+1\}} = \tau^0$; $s_n^{[n,n\oplus\ell]\{n,N+2\}} = A$, $b_{N+2}^{[n,n\oplus\ell]\{n,N+2\}} = Aq_n^{\{N+2,n\}}$; $s_{N+2}^{[n,n\oplus\ell]\{n\oplus\ell,N+2\}} = Aq_n^{\{N+2,n\}} - \tau^0$, $b_{n\oplus\ell}^{[n,n\oplus\ell]\{n\oplus\ell,N+2\}} = (Aq_n^{\{N+2,n\}} - \tau^0) q_{N+2}^{\{n\oplus\ell,N+2\}}$.

CYCLE 2, STEP 2:

- For $n, m \neq N + 2$, set $q_n^{\{m,n\}} = (1 - \delta^n)$. $q_n^{\{N+2,n\}} = (1 - \min[\delta^n, \gamma^n/\Omega A])(1 - \gamma^{N+2}/\Omega A)$, $q_{N+2}^{\{N+2,n\}} = 1$.

CYCLE 3, STEP 1: Repeat CYCLE 2, STEP 1.
CYCLE 3, STEP 2: Repeat CYCLE 2, STEP 2.
CONVERGENCE.

What is happening in this proposition? Scale economies are taking their course! Government expenditures in all goods markets in exchange for $N + 2$ (and large household demand to acquire $N + 2$ to finance tax payments) result in a large trading volume on the trading posts for good $N + 2$ versus $n = 1, \ldots, N$. Volume is large enough that scale economies kick in. The average cost pricing auctioneer adjusts prices, the bid–ask spread, to reflect the scale economies. The bid–ask spreads incurred on trading $m$ for $m \oplus \ell$ by way of good $N + 2$ become considerably narrower than on trading $m$ for $m \oplus \ell$ directly. The price system then directs each household to the market $\{m, N + 2\}$ where its endowment is traded against good $N + 2$. The household sells all its endowment there for $N + 2$ and trades $N + 2$ subsequently for tax payments and desired consumption. Scale economy has turned $N + 2$ from a mere tax payment coupon into 'money', the unique universally used common medium of exchange.

## 2 CONCLUSION: GOVERNMENT-ISSUED FIAT MONEY IS A NATURAL MONOPOLY

Fiat money is a puzzle in two dimensions: it is inherently worthless so why is it valuable? Why is it (and its close substitutes) the universal unique common medium of exchange? The answer to the first question is taxation payable in fiat money. The answer to the second comes from Chapters 6 and 7. Scale economies in transaction costs make money a natural monopoly. Government's large scale secures the monopoly to government's fiat instrument.

## NOTES

1.  This chapter is based on Starr (2003, 2004).
2.  See also Starr (1974) and Li and Wright (1998).
3.  (TCNC-T) is intended as a mnemonic for nonconvex transaction cost with taxation.

# 9. Efficient structure of exchange[1]

Monetary trade is found to be an efficient (cost-minimizing) trading structure when the fixed cost of maintaining a trading post is high, and the marginal cost of trading volume is low. An efficient array is then $N - 1$ active monetary trading posts, rather than $\frac{1}{2}N(N - 1)$ barter trading posts.

## 1 WHAT EXCHANGE STRUCTURE WOULD A CENTRAL PLANNER PRESCRIBE?

Chapters 4 through 8 have considered the notion of a general equilibrium trading arrangement in a trading post economy. Chapters 4 and 6 developed sufficient conditions so that a single common medium of exchange represented the general equilibrium pattern of trade. Conversely, Chapter 5 developed sufficient conditions so that a wide variety of trading posts remained active in equilibrium, a barter equilibrium. There is a long tradition in welfare economics noting the equivalence of market equilibrium to an efficient allocation of resources (Arrow, 1951). Can we make a similar claim for the market equilibrium structure of trade in a trading post economy?

This chapter will develop sufficient conditions, following Starr and Stinchcombe (1999), so that the monetary structure of trade is an efficient allocation. It is reassuring that these conditions closely parallel those where a market equilibrium is monetary. However, the emphasis here is that it may not be possible to rely on a decentralized market mechanism to achieve efficient allocation. Scale economies, the construct that drives monetization in Chapters 6 and 7, is the basis of monopoly. Hence it can be seen as an impediment to decentralization of efficient allocation. Note, particularly, that throughout those chapters the pricing model is average cost pricing, rather than the usual competitive model of marginal cost pricing.

Tobin (1980, p. 86) notes:

Social institutions like money are public goods. Models of . . . competitive markets and individual optimizing agents . . . are not well adapted to explaining the existence and quantity of public goods. . . . Both [money and language] are means of communication. The use of a particular language or a particular money by one individual increases its value to other actual or potential users. Increasing returns to scale, in this sense, limits the number of languages or moneys in a society and indeed explains the tendency for one basic language or money to monopolize the field.

Using the trading post model, the pairs of goods in active trade for one another will be described by a binary relation on the set of goods. A trading relation in which most goods are traded for one another will be nonmonetary; a trading relation in which there is a distinguished good for which most goods are traded but where most goods are not traded directly for one another is monetary with the distinguished good acting as money. The trading relation will be determined endogenously as a cost minimizer subject to fulfillment of demands and supplies. We seek to establish the observation that 'money buys goods and goods buy money but goods do not buy goods', Clower (1967, p. 5), as the result of optimization rather than as an assumption.

Walras (1874 [1954], p. 158) suggests that we think of trade taking place at a family of trading posts, one for each pair of goods: '$\frac{m(m-1)}{2}$ special markets each identified by a signboard indicating the names of the two commodities exchanged there as well as their prices or rates of exchange'. But $\frac{1}{2}N(N-1)$ may be far too many markets to be active in an efficient allocation. If there is a set-up cost on each pairwise trading post, it may be unneccessarily costly to maintain so many trading posts. When is the $N-1$-post system of monetary exchange preferable? We conceive of the problem of a central planner — not in deciding the allocation of all resources in the economy — but rather deciding on the structure of pairwise goods markets to be installed as a public good. The transaction and set-up costs of the markets are to be borne in common. What then is the cost-minimizing structure of markets consistent with the implementation of a general equilibrium allocation of commodities?

## 2 INITIAL CONDITIONS

Let there be $N$ goods, denoted $i = 1, 2, 3, \ldots, N$. Following the Arrow–Debreu model, prices will be denoted by $p \in P$, the unit simplex in $\mathbf{R}_+^N$. Note that for purposes of this chapter we dispense with the distinction between bid and ask prices. Let the typical trading household be denoted $h$, an element of the (finite) set of households $H$. For each $h \in H$, $z^h \in \mathbf{R}^N$ is $h$'s excess demand vector. We assume that $z^h$ fulfills household $h$'s budget constraint (9.1) and that market excess demands at $p$ clear (9.2).

Hence we assume:

$$p \cdot z^h = 0, \tag{9.1}$$

and

$$\sum_{h \in H} z^h = 0. \tag{9.2}$$

Let $\tilde{Z} \equiv [z^h]_{h \in H}$, where $[\cdot]_{h \in H}$ denotes the $\#H \times N$ matrix. Assume $\#H \geq 2$ and $\#N \geq 3$, and assume that all goods have nonnull supply and demand, to avoid trivially degenerate cases.

We describe an array of trading posts as a relation $\Psi$ on the $N$ commodities. The interpretation is that $i\Psi j$ if there is an (active) trading post for trade of $i$ and $j$. The notation $\neg i\Psi j$ denotes 'it is not the case that $i\Psi j$'. There is no trading post for trade of $i$ with $i$.

We shall restrict attention to trading post structures $\Psi$, connected in the sense that it is possible to trade each good $i$ for any other $j$ in a succession of trades using the trading posts available. Finally we require that the trading post where $i$ can be traded for $j$ is the trading post where $j$ can be traded for $i$.

**Definition**   A trading post structure $\Psi$ is connected in $m$ steps if it is possible to trade from each good $i$ to any other good $j$ in $m$ trades using the trading posts available in $\Psi$.

We seek now to describe the array of active trading posts as an optimizing decision.

## 3   TRADE PLANS

Household $h$'s trading plan is characterized by the $N \times N$ matrix $V^h = (v_{ij}^h)$. The intended interpretation is that $v_{ij}^h$ is $h$'s net receipt of $i$ in exchange for $j$: $v_{ij}^h < 0$ is a delivery of $i$ in exchange for $j$; $v_{ij}^h > 0$ is a receipt of $i$ in return for $j$. We expect each good traded to be paid for at the trading post by opposite delivery of the other good traded at the post:

$$p_i v_{ij}^h = -p_j v_{ji}^h. \tag{9.3}$$

Further, the trading plans should seek fully to implement $h$'s demands $z^h$:

$$\sum_j v_{ij}^h = z_i^h. \tag{9.4}$$

However, $h$'s trading plans should be consistent with the array of trading posts in active operation according to the relation $\Psi$. Thus:

$$v_{ij}^h \neq 0 \text{ only if } i\Psi j \text{ or } j\Psi i. \tag{9.5}$$

It is convenient to be able to distinguish $h$'s planned receipts ($v_{ij}^h > 0$) from its planned deliveries ($v_{ij}^h < 0$). To this end, let:

$$v_{ij}^{h+} = \begin{cases} v_{ij}^h \text{ if } v_{ij}^h \geq 0 \\ 0 \text{ if } v_{ij}^h < 0 \end{cases}, \tag{9.6}$$

and let:

$$v_{ij}^{h-} = \begin{cases} 0 \text{ if } v_{ij}^h \geq 0 \\ -v_{ij}^h \text{ if } v_{ij}^h < 0 \end{cases} \tag{9.7}$$

so that $h$'s planned receipts are $v_{ij}^{h+}$, planned deliveries are $v_{ij}^{h-}$, and $v_{ij}^h = v_{ij}^{h+} - v_{ij}^{h-}$. We discuss the endogenous determination of the $v_{ij}^h$ below.

To avoid an additional source of complexity, we do not impose an explicit condition of market clearing at each trading post separately. That is, there is no restriction that for each $i, j$ so that $i\Psi j$, $\Sigma_{h \in H} v_{ij}^h = 0$. It may occur at a solution that $\Sigma_{h \in H} v_{ij}^h \neq 0$. This reflects a notion that trading post $\{i, j\}$ will manage to deliver surpluses or acquire deficits from other trading posts without directly trading with individual households.

To illustrate how $\Psi$, the array of active trading posts, affects the pattern of trade, consider three very different cases:

- $E$ (the universal array) where there are $\frac{1}{2}N(N - 1)$ trading posts and all goods can trade against each other,
- a linear array with $N - 1$ trading posts and only prescribed pairs of goods trade against one another, each good trading against two other goods only, $i_1 \leftrightarrow i_2 \leftrightarrow \ldots i_N$, and
- monetary exchange, where there are $N - 1$ trading posts only but a single good, 'money', is one of the goods traded in each pair.

When $E$ is the trading array, all goods trade directly for one another. There are $\frac{1}{2}N(N - 1)$ trading posts in use. Each agent goes to the trading posts dealing in the combination of goods $ij$ where $i$ is one of his/her excess demands and $j$ is one of his/her excess supplies. His/her dollar (unit of account) volume of trade is precisely equal to the value of his excess supplies plus the value of his/her excess demands, that is, each excess supply is traded once for an excess demand.

In the linear array, there are $(N - 1)$ trading posts in use. There will typically be only two trading posts available where $j$, of which the trader has an excess supply, is traded. The trader chooses the one that will lead eventually to a post trading $i$ for which he/she has an excess demand. The trader goes to the first chosen trading post to deliver his/her excess supply and withdraw an equal value of the other good traded at the post. The trader retrades this good at the adjacent post for a third good, and then to an adjacent post for a fourth good, . . ., eventually arriving with a suitable supply at a post dealing in his/her desired excess demand for which he/she then trades. Trading volumes in this setting may be many times the value of excess demands, since each good may be retraded several times as a carrier of value between trading posts.

In the monetary array, there are $(N - 1)$ trading posts in use. The trader goes to each trading post dealing in a (nonmoney) good for which he/she has an excess supply and exchanges it for the money good. The trader then goes to the trading post where one of his/her demanded goods is traded and exchanges the money for the demanded good. The volume of trade is approximately two times the value of excess supplies plus excess demands (since each of these is traded once for an equal value of money). The number of active trading posts is the same as in the linear array, but the volume of trade is much smaller. The number of trading posts is $2/N^{ths}$ the number in the universal array and the gross volume of trade is larger.

Nonmonetary trade in the trading post model, even ignoring transaction costs, has a distinct problem that monetary trade can solve, market clearing at the trading post. Though markets clear for all goods (9.2), there is no guarantee that the flows at any single trading post will clear, that is, that $\Sigma_{h \in H} v_{ij}^h = 0$. This implies that there is an untreated issue of interpost trade in the nonmonetary model. However, monetary trade resolves this issue. All trade for good $i$ in a monetary trading array is at the trading post for $i$ and money. Hence in monetary trade (9.2) implies purchases equal sales at the trading post. This follows simply because monetary trade is exchange of excess demands and supplies for money and (9.2) guarantees that the excess demands and supplies clear.

# 4   THE CENTRAL PROBLEM OF EFFICIENT EXCHANGE

How should an economy arrange its bilateral trade? Some arrays of trading posts may be more costly than others to arrange, sustain, and use for trade.

In particular, if a choice of $\Psi$ (like the linear array) meant that most trades had to go through a circuitous trading sequence, or an alternative choice (like $E$) meant that many redundant trading posts were kept open, then these might represent excessively costly, inefficient choices of trading array. Is it efficient or desirable to organize trade as monetary trade? Given $p \in P$, $z^h$ fulfilling (9.1), (9.2), then an optimal choice of $\Psi$ would minimize the cost of $\widetilde{Z}$, $\Psi$ subject to (9.3)−(9.5).

For all $i, j \in N$, pairs with $i \neq j$, let $\alpha_{ij}$ be a fixed cost of running the trading post for the pair of goods $ij$. Because we assume that the trading post where $i$ is traded for $j$ is the same as the trading post where $j$ is traded for $i$, it is natural to assume that $\alpha_{ij} = \alpha_{ji}$. For $i \in N$, let $\beta_i$ be the marginal cost of flows of good $i$. Let $\widetilde{\alpha}$ and $\widetilde{\beta}$ and be the vectors of $\alpha$'s and $\beta$'s. We study cost functions of the form:

$$C(\Psi, \widetilde{Z}; \widetilde{\alpha}, \widetilde{\beta}) = \sum_{i>j, i\Psi j} \alpha_{ij} + \sum_{i>j} \beta_i \left[ \sum_{h \in H} v_{ij}^{h+} + \sum_{h \in H} v_{ij}^{h-} \right], \qquad (9.8)$$

where $v_{ij}^h$ for all $h \in H$ is chosen to optimize $h$'s decision for given $\Psi, \widetilde{\beta}$. Households choose their planned trades, $V^h$, in response to $\Psi$, $\widetilde{Z}$, and (potentially) to $\widetilde{\beta}$. Household $h$ chooses trading pattern, $V^h$ to be consistent with (9.3)−(9.7), and to minimize:

$$\sum_{i>j} \beta_i (v_{ij}^{h+} + v_{ij}^{h-}), \qquad (9.9)$$

where each $\beta_i > 0$.

# 5 SMALL FIXED COSTS

In this section we consider cost functions for which the marginal costs of trade flows are large and the fixed costs are negligible. Section 6 considers the opposite case of negligible marginal costs.

Here, total costs are virtually linear in the quantity of goods traded. The cost-minimizing trading post structure is $E(\widetilde{Z})$, the array of trading posts containing all pairs of goods which at least one household would like to trade,

$$E(\widetilde{Z}) = \{ (i, j): \text{for some } h \in H, sgn(z_i^h) \neq sgn(z_j^h) \}. \qquad (9.10)$$

$E(\widetilde{Z})$ is the universal relation $E$ minus all those pairs of goods that no household might want to trade.

The excess demand array $\widetilde{Z}$ is *indecomposable* if it cannot be partitioned into a block-diagonal array. That is, the economy is indecomposable if its households cannot be partitioned into two disjoint subsets each of which can fully fulfill its demands and supplies without trading with the other of the two subsets.

The trading post array $E(\widetilde{Z})$ is the cost-minimizing solution in this case because with any other system, some trader(s) would be obliged to trade indirectly, increasing the volume of trade flows and hence increasing costs by a nonnegligible amount. In particular, a system of monetary trade with all flows through a single good $k$ cannot be optimal, except in a trivial case where all households have either an excess supply of only one good and that single good is $k$, or an excess demand for only one good and that single good is $k$. We wish to describe the efficient trading post arrays, $\Psi$, as cost-minimizing solutions for the following problem,

$$\min_{\Psi} C(\Psi, \widetilde{Z}; \widetilde{\alpha}, \widetilde{\beta}) \text{ subject to } \Psi \text{ symmetric and connected in } m \text{ steps. (9.11)}$$

Here $m$ is a positive integer indicating the maximum number of trading posts at which the household may need to trade successively in order to exchange good $i$ for good $j$. In other words, the constraints are that $\Psi$ be symmetric and connected in $m$ or fewer steps. The property $m$-connectedness is intended as a proxy for the costs of many successive trades.

**Proposition 1**  Consider $\Psi$ solving (9.11) for $C$ described in (9.8). If $\widetilde{\alpha} > 0$ and $\widetilde{\alpha} \approx 0$ and $\widetilde{\beta} > 0$, then for indecomposable $\widetilde{Z} \neq 0$, $E(\widetilde{Z})$ is the cost-minimizing choice of $\Psi$.

**Demonstration**  Consider first household $h$'s decision to choose the trading pattern $v_{ij}^h$. By assumption, $h$ is minimizing $\frac{1}{2}\Sigma_{i,j}(\beta_i + \beta_j) \cdot (v_{ij}^{h+} + v_{ij}^{h-})$. Suppose that it is possible to re-route a quantity of trade $\varepsilon$ between goods 1 and 2 through good 3. This leads to a change of $\frac{1}{2}[(\beta_1 + \beta_2)\varepsilon - (\beta_1 + \beta_3)\varepsilon + (\beta_2 + \beta_3)\varepsilon] = \beta_2\varepsilon$ in the objective function. Thus, for any proposed route structure, moving in a direction of more direct trade, $\varepsilon < 0$, lowers the function to be minimized. Thus, household $h$ will choose direct trade if possible.

Turning now to the economy-wide problem, the above argument shows that the most direct possible trade also solves the problem of minimizing the total cost of flows. Because $\widetilde{\alpha} \approx 0$, the cost of any given trading post that some household might want to use is negligible in comparison to the saving to be had by including it in the trading post array. Finally, because $\widetilde{\alpha} > 0$, we save by omitting unused trading posts, and the result is $E(\widetilde{Z})$.
QED

# 6 HIGH FIXED COSTS, SMALL MARGINAL COSTS AND MONETARY TRADE

We now examine the implications of negligible marginal costs, a situation where the fixed costs of trading posts are decisive, formally, $\tilde{\beta} \simeq 0$ and $\tilde{\alpha} > 0$. In this case, the minimal total cost is achieved by establishing the minimal number of trading posts consistent with connecting all commodities with the minimal number of trading posts. This is $(N - 1)$. The trading posts could then be in the form of a line, $i_1 \leftrightarrow i_2 \leftrightarrow \ldots \leftrightarrow i_N$, a hub-and-spoke array (monetary trade), or a variety of alternative configurations.

Line structures of trading post arrays have an obvious drawback from the point of view of the traders; a single exchange of one good for another in a line array might involve as many as $N - 1$ distinct transactions as an excess supply was traded for each of a succession of intervening goods with active trading posts, eventually achieving the good in excess demand. In a cycle this trade might require $\frac{1}{2}(N - 1)$ transactions. Our proxy for this cost is the restriction that traders need make no more than $m$ distinct transactions in order to complete a two good (one supply, one demand) trade. If $m = 1$, then the only connected trading post structure is a system of trading posts for every commodity pair, $E$. The case $m = 2$ corresponds to retrading more than once being prohibitively expensive. In this context, with low variable costs and fixed costs approximately uniform, we are led to monetary trade networks with a single money, Proposition 2.

**Definition**  A monetary trade system with a single money $k \in N$ is a relation $\Psi$ such that $i\Psi k$ and $k\Psi i$ for all $i \neq k$, and $\neg i\Psi j$ if neither $i$ nor $j$ is equal to $k$.

Note that monetary trade systems with a single money are connected and they have $(N - 1)$ trading posts in them.

**Proposition 2**  If $\#N \geq 3$, $\tilde{Z}$ is indecomposable, $\tilde{\beta} \simeq 0$, $\tilde{\alpha} > 0, \alpha_{ij}$ approximately equal for all $i, j$, then the unique cost-minimizing relations connected in two steps $\Psi$ are monetary trade systems with a single money.

**Proof**  Because $\tilde{\beta} \simeq 0$ and $\alpha_{ij} > 0$ are approximately equal, it is sufficient to show that monetary trade systems with one money are the only solutions to the problem:

$$\min_{\Psi} \#\{\{i, j\} | i\Psi j\} \text{ s.t. } \Psi \text{ connected in two steps and symmetric.} \quad (9.12)$$

Monetary trade systems with a single money satisfy the constraint and have $(N - 1)$ trading posts in them. It is trivial that this is the minimum number of posts in a connected system. QED

If the $\alpha_{ij}$ values differ substantially among themselves, then it is easy to see that the result of Proposition 2 can fail. The fixed costs of trading posts, $\alpha_{ij}$, may vary across the posts $\{i, j\}$ so that for each choice of 'money', a common medium of exchange, there are some high-cost posts and some low-cost posts in use. Then the low-cost solution will not be hub−spoke with a single hub, but more complex, to link low-cost pairs together in a connected array.

The argument above has concentrated on a single common medium of exchange for an indecomposable economy. Obviously, if the economy is decomposable then a multiplicity of moneys can occur. Thus distinct national currencies, each prevailing separately, could be the outcome of a similar analysis.

## 7 WHY IS MONEY LIKE CHICAGO'S O'HARE AIRPORT?

This chapter is based on Starr and Stinchcombe (1999). The character of the cost structure is formally very similar to the cost structure in the transportation models of Hendricks et al. (1992) and Starr and Stinchcombe (1992). Starr and Stinchcombe analyzed the cost-minimizing structure of airline route systems. There are $N$ cities to be linked by airline routes.

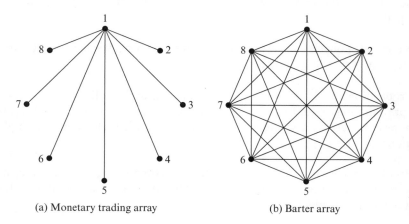

(a) Monetary trading array      (b) Barter array

*Figure 9.1   The hub-and-spoke spider diagram*

Direct flights between each city pair implies $\frac{1}{2}N(N-1)$ air routes. A hub-and-spoke network uses only $N-1$, however at the cost of causing some passengers to travel redundant mileage and to incur the delays of changes of plane. The saving in routes is efficient if there are strong set-up costs on each route and if the costs of extra mileage are correspondingly low. A transportation cost function displaying sufficient scale economy causes the route structure of the airlines to minimize costs for a given level of service with a hub-and-spoke network. All travel there passes through the hub to take advantage of scale economies (declining average cost per passenger) at the level of a single flight. This observation gave rise to an exam question at the University of California, San Diego: 'Why is money like Chicago's O'Hare airport?'.

## 8  CONCLUSION

'When is a hub–spoke airline system more efficient than a direct flight system?' is the same question as 'When is monetary trade with a unique monetary instrument more efficient than direct barter trade?'. The answer is: When pairwise links have high fixed costs, but the marginal costs of (trading or passenger) volume are low. In the diagram above, when is the spider-shaped array more practical than the star-shaped array? When $N-1$ links are more practical than $\frac{1}{2}N(N-1)$. Monetary trade saves on the fixed costs of maintaining a large array of specialized trading links, of each good $i$ for each counterpart $j$.

## NOTE

1. This chapter is based on Starr and Stinchcombe (1999).

# 10. Microfoundations of Jevons's double coincidence condition[1]

Jevons's double coincidence of wants condition for barter trade is inconsistent with the Arrow–Debreu general equilibrium model. But it can be derived from more elementary transaction cost properties. Suppose each household experiences a set-up cost on entering an additional trading post. Existence and local uniqueness of commodity money in equilibrium can follow from the scale economy implied by the household set-up cost. Jevons's double coincidence condition is an outcome of transaction cost structure in general equilibrium.

## 1   INTRODUCTION

Jevons (1875, p. 3) observes:

> [In monetary] sale and purchase . . . one of the articles exchanged is intended to be held only for a short time, until it is parted with in a second act of exchange. The object which thus temporarily intervenes in sale and purchase is money. At first sight it might seem that the use of money only doubles the trouble, by making two exchanges necessary where one was sufficient; but a slight analysis of the difficulties inherent in simple barter shows that the balance of trouble lies quite in the opposite direction . . .
>
> The first difficulty in barter is to find two persons whose disposable possessions mutually suit each other's wants. There may be many people wanting, and many possessing those things wanted; but to allow an act of barter, there must be a double coincidence, which will rarely happen.

Jevons's statement appears sound, but we should recognize how completely it is at odds with a conventional Arrow–Debreu general equilibrium model (Arrow and Debreu, 1954; Debreu, 1959). In the Arrow–Debreu model, there are no transaction costs. Each agent has goods he/she is trying to sell − goods he/she does not want. There is no reason why the agent should decline − at prevailing prices − to accept one good he/she does not want in exchange for another he/she does not want. In a model with linear transaction costs, the agent should be willing to make such a trade at a discount reflecting the costs of exchange. And how does money come into the array – a commodity asymmetrically acceptable? If all goods carry zero transaction costs or similar linear transaction costs there is no advantage in accepting money, a commonly traded good (that one does not want) in order to retrade it, instead of another that a fellow trader has in excess supply.

## 1.1 A Distinctive Modeling Approach

In this chapter, we shall try to determine the structure of individual incentives or transaction costs that results in a general equilibrium pattern of trade that follows the Jevons description. This chapter takes a distinctive approach. Throughout the rest of this volume, transaction costs are modeled as though they were incurred by the trading post and then passed on to households in the form of a bid–ask spread. That approach does not easily lead to why Jevons's condition makes sense. Transaction costs will here be modeled as incurred at the level of the individual household. This is the approach taken in Kurz (1974) and in Heller and Starr (1976). Transactions are assumed to be a costly activity, in utility terms, at the household level. That is not sufficient in itself to allow them to be priced in a bid–ask spread. The notion to be derived here is that when there is a common medium of exchange, good $n^*$, and transaction costs are sufficiently low, that it is worthwhile to sell endowment and buy desired goods through this commodity money.

For each good, there are $N - 1$ trading posts where it can be traded. Assuming absence of double coincidence of wants, at some there is a latent demand, at others a latent supply. The pricing issue is what are prevailing prices at the nonmonetary trading posts. Goods in excess supply at some barter trading posts must be priced low enough to discourage their owners from selling there, but high enough that prospective demanders are also discouraged. Goods in excess demand at a barter trading post must be priced high enough that those desiring them will prefer to purchase at the monetary posts but low enough that prospective suppliers prefer to trade at the monetary posts. The spread between low prices at excess supply posts and high prices at excess demand posts (for any given good) must be narrow enough to discourage arbitrage. That array of prices, if it can be sustained in equilibrium, is the pricing array that results in Jevons's double coincidence condition.

The household faces a tradeoff. Assume that the household incurs a transaction cost, a set-up cost in utility terms, for each trading post at which it transacts. The minimum number of trading posts it can enter is reflected by the number of buying and selling pairs of goods it is interested in. If it has one good for sale and several for purchase, the minimum number of posts it can enter is equal to the number of desired purchases. But those markets may price the household's selling good at a discount. Conversely, if there is a common medium of exchange, commodity money, discounts may be smaller at the monetary trading posts but trading there will add to the number of trading posts the household enters with consequent personal cost. Then the problem is to describe $N(N - 1)$ general equilibrium bid prices so that the equilibrium pattern of trade is monetary and barter though possible will be inactive, absent a double coincidence of wants.

## 2  HOUSEHOLDS

For simplicity, let the population of households be identified with the $N$ commodities. Each household, $h$, will be designated as a type shown by one of $h = 1, 2, \ldots, N$. A household of type $h$ then is endowed with $A$ units of good $h$. We assume a large economy with the same large number of households of each type $h = 1, 2, \ldots, N$. The economy is large enough to overcome the limited size of each household's demands. There is no non-price rationing in equilibrium. Individual households seek to economize on the number of trading posts they use.

   Households formulate their trading plans deciding how much of each good to trade at each pairwise trading post. This leads to the usual messy notation:

   $b_n^{h,\{i,j\}}$ = planned purchase of good $n$ by household $h$ at trading post $\{i, j\}$.

   $s_n^{h,\{i,j\}}$ = planned sale of good $n$ by household $h$ at trading post $\{i, j\}$.

There is some excess generality in this notation, since the only goods $n$ actually transacted at $\{i, j\}$ are $i$ and $j$. This point is formalized in condition (T.i) of the trading post balance constraints in Chapter 3.

   The notation $\oplus$ is defined in the following way. For any $n, j = 1, 2, \ldots, N$ $n \oplus j \equiv n + j$ if $n + j \leq N$, or $\equiv n + j - N$ if $n + j > N$. That is, $n \oplus j$ is $n + j$ mod $N$.

   In order to emphasize the absence of double coincidence of wants in the array of original endowments and tastes, we shall assume household $h°$ is endowed with good $h° = 1, 2, \ldots, N$ and prefers $h° \oplus 1, h° \oplus 2, h° \oplus 3$. Let $N \geq 10$. We can specify utility functions and market prices so that a market clearing condition is fulfilled: for each good the amount demanded from the market equals the amount supplied to the market. But for any two households, and on any single trading post, there is no double coincidence of wants. Let $\ell > 0$. Then the typical household's utility function is:

$$u^h(x^h) = \min [x^h_{h\oplus1}, x^h_{h\oplus2}, x^h_{h\oplus3}] - \ell \cdot [\#\{b^{h\{i,j\}}_i \neq 0 \mid 1 \leq i, j \leq N\}]^a$$

$$\alpha > 1, \ell > 0,$$

where for household $h$ of type $n$, for all goods $m \neq n$, $x^h_m \equiv \Sigma_{\{i,j\}}(b^{h\{i,j\}}_m - s^{h\{i,j\}}_m)$.

The concluding term in the expression for $u^h$ reflects the notion that the household incurs a personal transaction cost for each trading post where the household conducts active trade. The cost starts at $\ell$ for the first post used, and increases per unit with each additional trading post used. Thus the household seeks to manage its trades to satisfy trading needs, represented as the first term on the RHS, while restricting the number of trading posts where it maintains activity. Under the budget balance constraint, any trading post where $h$ has a buying transaction is also a post where it has a selling transaction. Thus the transaction cost notation in $u^h$ above, counting only trading posts where $h$ buys, includes equivalently an implicit count for posts where $h$ sells.

In addition to the usual trading post balance constraints on bilateral trade (in Chapter 3), (T.i), (T.ii), (T.iii), a quantity limit on arbitrage trade is useful:

(T.iv) For each household $h$, $s^{h\{i,j\}}_i \leq A$ for all $i, j$.

Household $h$ faces the array of prices $q^{\{i,j\}}_i$, $q^{\{i,j\}}_j$ and chooses $s^{h\{i,j\}}_m$ and $b^{h\{i,j\}}_m$, $m = i, j$, to maximize $u^h(x^h)$ subject to (T.i), (T.ii), (T.iii), (T.iv). That is, $h$ chooses which pairwise markets to transact in and a transaction plan to optimize utility, subject to a multiplicity of pairwise budget constraints. (T.iv) limits the size of household sales to the scale of endowment. This represents a limit on the scope of arbitrage in a large economy. In the absence of (T.iv) in a large economy, an arbitrageur could undertake arbitrarily large transactions, effectively overcoming the scale economy implicit in the transaction cost structure. The economic rationale for (T.iv) is credit rationing; an excessively large transaction (in this single-period economy) necessarily implies an extension of credit during the transaction process to the large transactor.

A competitive equilibrium consists of $q^{o\{i,j\}}_i$, $q^{o\{i,j\}}_j$, $1 \leq i, j \leq N$, so that: for each household $h$, there is a utility-optimizing plan $b^{oh\{i,j\}}_n$, $s^{oh\{i,j\}}_n$ (subject to T.i, T.ii, T.iii, T.iv), so that for each $\{i,j\}$, $\Sigma_h b^{oh\{i,j\}}_i = \Sigma_h s^{oh\{i,j\}}_i$, all $i \neq j$.

An equilibrium is said to be 'monetary' with a commodity money, $\mu$, if all transactions are at trading posts including μ and μ is the only good that a household will both buy and sell.

## 3    A MONETARY EQUILIBRIUM

We seek sufficient transaction cost conditions in an example so that there is an equilibrium pattern of trade where all trade (except that displaying a double coincidence of wants) goes through a common medium of exchange, a commodity money. The strategy is to consider three possible patterns of trade by households: barter, monetary trade, and arbitrage on the barter markets. We then find trading post break-even prices so that barter and monetary trade are equally successful and so that monetary and arbitrage trade are equally successful. Based on the break-even prices, we can find pricing so that monetary trade is the most rewarding strategy. Barter trade by the household consists of trading on three trading posts: endowed good versus the three desired goods. Monetary trade consists of trading on four trading posts: endowed good versus commodity money, commodity money versus three desired goods. Arbitrage may consist of trade on five trading posts: endowed good versus a second good, second good versus commodity money, commodity money versus three desired goods. Arbitrage may alternatively include a nonendowed good: sale of an overpriced good for an underpriced good, sale of the underpriced good for money, repurchase of the overpriced good for money (to deliver the initial sale), purchase of desired goods for money.

In the case where there is a common medium of exchange, commodity money, start by assuming that it trades one for one with each of the other goods, fixing money's price at unity. Since all goods enter symmetrically in agents' utility functions, the example below will assume symmetric pricing. Goods 2, 3, and 4 are desired by type 1 households. Goods 3, 4, and 5 are desired by type 2 households. . . . Goods 1, 2, and 3 are desired by type $N$ households. Hence we assume $q_i^{\{i,i\oplus1\}} = q_i^{\{i,i\oplus2\}} = q_i^{\{i,i\oplus3\}}$ for $1 \le i \le N$ (with the exception of the case where $i, i \oplus 1, i \oplus 2$, or $i \oplus 3$ is the commodity money and hence the price is unity).

At trading posts $\{i, i \oplus 1\}, \{i, i \oplus 2\}, \{i, i \oplus 3\}$, good $i$ is in supply and $i \oplus 1, i \oplus 2, i \oplus 3$, are in demand. Hence $i$ trades at a discount; $i \oplus 1, i \oplus 2$, and $i \oplus 3$ trade at a premium.

### 3.1    Better than Break-even Prices: Pricing where Monetary Trade Is Superior to Barter

Denote the price of the typical nonmonetary good owned by household of type $i$ in exchange for a desired good under barter, $q_i^{\{i,i\oplus1\}}$, by $q$. By symmetry we take this value to be the same across all nonmonetary goods. We would like to figure out the value of $q$ so that a type $i$ household is better satisfied trading in monetary fashion. In the following expression, the left-hand side is the utility of the typical household under barter trade; the right-hand side is the utility of a similar household under monetary trade. The inequality is intended to characterize $q°$ so that monetary trade is preferable to barter:

$$q\frac{A}{3} - 3^{\alpha}\ell < \frac{A}{3} - 4^{\alpha}\ell. \tag{10.1}$$

Solving for the barter price $q°$ where monetary trade is superior we get that

$$q° < 1 - \frac{3}{A}(4^{\alpha} - 3^{\alpha})\ell. \tag{10.2}$$

Thus, when barter is sufficiently costly, monetary trade will be superior. Low values of $q_i^{\{i,i\oplus 1\}}$, the barter value of good $i$, drive trade to using money. How low can $q$ go? If $q$ gets too low, the price will induce arbitrage buying. That limit is investigated next.

In the following expression, the left-hand side is the utility of the typical household under monetary trade; the right-hand side is the utility of a similar household performing the following arbitrage: good $i$ for $j$, $j$ for money, money for $i \oplus 1$, $i \oplus 2$, $i \oplus 3$. The size of the arbitrageur's transaction is limited by (T.iv). The inequality is intended to characterize $q^{\dagger}$, the floor on prices set by the possibility of arbitrage:

$$\frac{A}{3} - 4^{\alpha}\ell > \frac{A}{3q} - 5^{\alpha}\ell. \tag{10.3}$$

Solving for the lower bound on the barter price $q$, $q^{\dagger}$, where monetary trade is superior, we find we find:

$$q > q^{\dagger} = \left[1 + \left(\frac{3}{A}(5^{\alpha} - 4^{\alpha})\ell\right)\right]^{-1} \tag{10.4}$$

Note that this treatment of arbitrage, starting with the endowed good and hence adding only one additional trading post's cost, dominates the alternative of arbitrage with a nonendowed good (adding three trading posts' costs). Hence the value of $q^{\dagger}$ above is sufficient characterization of arbitrage-free pricing.

### 3.1.1 Sustainable pricing in a monetary equilibrium

Thus monetary trade will be sustained where $q° > q_i^{\{i,i\oplus 1\}} > q^{\dagger}$. This interval is nonempty when:

$$1 > 1 - \frac{3}{A}(4^\alpha - 3^\alpha)\ell > 0, \tag{10.5}$$

and

$$1 - \frac{3}{A}(4^\alpha - 3^\alpha)\ell > \left[1 + \left(\frac{3}{A}(5^\alpha - 4^\alpha)\ell\right)\right]^{-1} \tag{10.6}$$

(to discourage arbitrage) or equivalently when:

$$\left[1 - \frac{3}{A}(4^\alpha - 3^\alpha)\ell\right]\left[1 + \left(\frac{3}{A}(5^\alpha - 4^\alpha)\ell\right)\right] > 1. \tag{10.7}$$

(10.5) says that the transaction costs of monetization are not in themselves overwhelming. The inequality (10.7) will generally be true for $\alpha > 1$ and $\ell > 0$, such that (10.5) is true.

### 3.2  Monetary Equilibrium Pricing

Let $q^\circ > q^* > q^\dagger$. Table 10.1 presents the equilibrium prices for a monetary equilibrium. Good $n^*$ is the commodity money. The choice of good $n^*$ is arbitrary, since all goods in this example are symmetric, but it is treated asymmetrically as the common medium of exchange. $q_i^{\{i,n^*\}} = 1$ and $q_{n^*}^{\{n^*,j\}} = 1$. The typical price, $q_i^{\{i,j\}}$, is the price for good $i$ at trading post $\{i, j\}$. For $i, i \oplus 1, i \oplus 2, i \oplus 3 \neq n^*$, we have $q^\dagger < q^* = q_i^{\{i,i\oplus1\}} < q^\circ$, $q^\dagger < q^* = q_i^{\{i,i\oplus2\}} < q^\circ$, and $q^\dagger < q^* = q_i^{\{i,i\oplus3\}} < q^\circ$. Conversely, $q_{i\oplus1}^{\{i,i\oplus1\}} = [q_i^{\{i,i\oplus1\}}]^{-1}$. At these prices all trade proceeds through the trading posts trading $n^*$.

The monetary equilibrium pricing in Table 10.1 reflects the double coincidence of wants condition on direct trade. Good $i$ is priced at a discount at trading posts $\{i, i \oplus 1\}$, $\{i, i \oplus 2\}$, $\{i, i \oplus 3\}$ and at a premium at posts $\{i, (i - 4) \oplus 1\}$, $\{i, (i - 4) \oplus 2\}$, $\{i, (i - 4) \oplus 3\}$. The assumed pattern of endowment and preferences means that at no trading post will there be mutually satisfactory barter trades. Double coincidence of wants is assumed absent. Then households do not trade their endowments for a good they desire; equilibrium prices and transaction costs make that unattractive. They trade the endowment for a common medium of exchange and then trade that good for desired consumption. The pattern of trade is an outcome, not an assumption, of the example, reflecting the structure of transaction cost.

Table 10.1  *Jevons's monetary equilibrium trading post bid prices*

| Selling: | 1 | 2 | 3 | ... | $n^*$ | ... | $N-1$ | $N$ |
|---|---|---|---|---|---|---|---|---|
| **Buying:** | | | | | | | | |
| 1 | X | $q_2^{\{1,2\}} = [q^*]^{-1}$ | $q_3^{\{1,3\}} = [q^*]^{-1}$ | ... | 1 | ... | $q_{N-1}^{\{1,N-1\}} = q^*$ | $q_N^{\{1,N\}} = q^*$ |
| 2 | $q_1^{\{2,1\}} = q^*$ | X | $q_3^{\{2,3\}} = [q^*]^{-1}$ | ... | 1 | ... | $q_{N-1}^{\{2,N-1\}} = q^*$ | $q_N^{\{2,N\}} = q^*$ |
| 3 | $q_1^{\{3,1\}} = q^*$ | $q_2^{\{3,2\}} = q^*$ | X | ... | 1 | ... | $q_{N-1}^{\{3,N-1\}}$ | $q_N^{\{3,N\}} = q^*$ |
| ... | ⋮ | ⋮ | ⋮ | ⋮ | X | ⋮ | ⋮ | ⋮ |
| $n^*$ | 1 | 1 | 1 | 1 | X | 1 | 1 | 1 |
| ... | ⋮ | ⋮ | ⋮ | ⋮ | 1 | ⋮ | ⋮ | ⋮ |
| $N-1$ | $q_1^{\{N-1,1\}} = [q^*]^{-1}$ | $q_2^{\{N-1,2\}} = [q^*]^{-1}$ | $q_3^{\{N-1,3\}}$ | ... | 1 | ... | X | $q_N^{\{N-1,N\}} = q^*$ |
| $N$ | $q_1^{\{N,1\}} = [q^*]^{-1}$ | $q_2^{\{N,2\}} = [q^*]^{-1}$ | $q_3^{\{N,3\}} = [q^*]^{-1}$ | ... | 1 | ... | $q_{N-1}^{\{N,N-1\}} = q^*$ | X |

## 4 CONCLUSION

What was Jevons thinking? The pattern of transaction cost posited here (a set-up cost on each additional trading post a household uses) provides a price-theoretic foundation for Jevons's assumption: 'to allow an act of barter, there must be a double coincidence'.

## NOTE

1. This chapter is based on Starr (2010).

# 11. Commodity money equilibrium in a convex trading post economy[1]

Sufficient conditions for existence of general equilibrium with commodity money in the trading post model of Chapter 3 are developed in this chapter. $N$ commodities are traded at $\frac{1}{2}N(N-1)$ commodity-pairwise trading posts. Trade is a resource-using activity located in optimizing firms recovering transaction costs through the spread between bid and ask prices. Budget constraints, enforced at each trading post separately, imply demand for a carrier of value between trading posts. General equilibrium exists under conventional convexity and continuity conditions while structuring the price space to account for distinct bid and ask prices. Commodity money flows are identified as the difference between gross and net inter-post trades.

## 1 THE ABSENCE OF MONEY IN THE ARROW–DEBREU MODEL

It is well known that the Arrow–Debreu model of Walrasian general equilibrium cannot account for money.

One of the leading achievements of the Arrow–Debreu model is to characterize and demonstrate existence of the general equilibrium under a broad array of weak sufficient conditions. Though this volume presents a variety of examples of general equilibrium in the trading post model, they are just examples. Is there a family of weak sufficient conditions so that the trading post model has an equilibrium? Is there then a role for medium of exchange, a commodity money?

What is the problem with the Arrow–Debreu model? Why can it not account for money? There are two big reasons. One is that all trade takes place at a single exchange, so there is no role for a carrier of value between trades. The second is that the markets perform many of the financial functions themselves: futures and contingent commodity markets perform capital market and insurance functions – saving, investment, and precautionary demands take nonmonetary forms.

This chapter will present a conventional weak (that is, with broad coverage) family of sufficient conditions so that the trading post model has a general equilibrium and a well-defined demand for commodity money. The formal structure of the proof is similar to the proof in an Arrow–Debreu model, but the price space and firm and household choice fully reflect the trading post structure of the model.

# 2   GENERAL EQUILIBRIUM OF THE TRADING POST MODEL

The simple example of Chapter 4 demonstrated that the trading post model can generate a market-clearing equilibrium where one good acts as a common medium of exchange. An example is suggestive, but an example is not enough to satisfy a demanding theorist. We would be much happier with general results: what are sufficient conditions for a trading post model to have market-clearing equilibrium prices, like an Arrow–Debreu model? Can we generally identify goods acting as media of exchange? This chapter should begin to answer those questions, and to do so with considerable generality. The issue whether the resulting allocation is Pareto efficient is treated in Chapter 12.

The trading post model is intended to provide a parsimonious[2] addition to the Arrow–Debreu model sufficient to generate a theory of money. The monetary structure of trade is shown to be a consequence of price theory. The medium (media) of exchange is (are) a consequence of general equilibrium, not a separate assumption.

## 2.1   Structure of the Trading Post Model

In the trading post model, presented in Chapter 3, transactions take place at commodity pairwise trading posts with budget constraints (you pay for what you get in commodity terms) enforced at each post. Prices − bid (wholesale) and ask (retail) − are quoted as commodity rates of exchange. Trade is arranged by firms, typically buying at bid prices and selling at ask prices, incurring costs (resources used up in the transaction process) and recouping them through the bid–ask spread. Market equilibrium occurs when bid and ask prices at each trading post have adjusted so that all trading posts clear.

## 2.2   Structure of the Proof

The structure of the proof of existence of general equilibrium follows the approach of Arrow and Debreu (1954), Debreu (1959), and Starr (1997).

The usual assumptions of continuity, convexity (traditional but by no means innocuous in this context), and no free lunch/irreversibility are used. The price space at a trading post for exchange of one good at bid price for another at ask price is the unit 1-simplex, allowing any possible nonnegative relative price ratio. The price space for the economy as a whole then is a Cartesian product of unit 1-simplices. The attainable set of trading post transactions is compact. As in Arrow and Debreu (1954), the model considers transaction plans of firms and households artificially bounded in a compact set including the attainable set as a proper subset. Price adjustment to a fixed point with market clearing leads to equilibrium of the artificially bounded economy. But the artificial bounds are not a binding constraint in equilibrium. The equilibrium of the artificially bounded economy is as well an equilibrium of the original economy.

The multiplicity of prices, each good priced at $N - 1$ different trading posts, implies that the notion of profit or value maximization is not well defined, so it is difficult to determine an appropriate maximand for the firm. A very general maximand on net trades, including prevailing prices as an argument, expresses the objective of the firm. In the case where profits are well-defined, the maximand includes profit as a special case.

## 2.3   Conclusion: The Medium/Media of Exchange

The general equilibrium specifies each household and firm's trading plan. At the conclusion of trade, each has achieved a net trade. Gross trades include trading activity that goes to paying for acquisitions and accepting payment for sales rather than directly implementing desired net trades. It is easy to calculate gross trades and net trades at equilibrium. For households, the difference — gross trades minus net trades — represents trading activity in carriers of value between trades, media of exchange (perhaps including some arbitrage). Since firms perform a market-making function within trading posts, identification of media of exchange used by firms is not so straightforward. After netting out intra-post trades, the remaining difference between inter-post gross and net trades represents the firms' trade flows of media of exchange. In some examples (Chapter 4) the medium of exchange may be a single specialized commodity (the common medium of exchange). The approach of this chapter provides a Walrasian general equilibrium theory of (commodity) money as a medium of exchange. It is sufficiently general to include both a single common medium of exchange and many goods simultaneously acting as media of exchange.

When will media of exchange actually be used in the trading post economy? Two conditions seem to be sufficient: desirability of trade, net of transaction costs; and absence of double coincidence of wants. The logic is simple. If trade is desirable at prevailing equilibrium prices (net of transaction costs including the transaction cost of media of exchange) and there is no double coincidence of wants, then in order for trade to proceed fulfilling the budget constraint at each trading post separately, media of exchange will be used as carriers of value between trading posts. However, the absence of double coincidence of wants depends on (endogenously determined) prevailing prices as well as endowments and technology. It is difficult to characterize necessary and sufficient initial conditions so that absence of double coincidence will be fulfilled. Absence of double coincidence is endogenously determined by the interaction of endowments, tastes, technology, and transaction costs. Hence the reliance on simple illustrative examples[3] in Chapter 12.

Conversely, there are two cases where trading post equilibria will have no use of media of exchange: full double coincidence of wants (subject to direct trade experiencing no higher transaction costs than indirect trade); and a no-trade equilibrium. Again, necessary and sufficient conditions, a priori, to fulfill these characteristics are not immediately evident. No-trade equilibria may be the result of a Pareto-efficient endowment or of prohibitive transaction costs.

## 3   TRADING POSTS AND PRICES

There are $N$ tradeable goods denoted 1, 2, . . ., $N$. They are traded for one another pairwise at trading posts. $\{i, j\}$ (or equivalently $\{j, i\}$) denotes the trading post where goods $i$ and $j$ are traded for one another. There are $\frac{1}{2}N(N-1)$ distinct trading posts. Goods are traded directly for one another without distinguishing any single good as 'money'.

Let $\Delta$ represent the unit 1-simplex. At trading post $\{i, j\}$, the (relative) ask price of good $i$ and (relative) bid price of good $j$ are represented as $p^{\{i,j\}} \equiv (\alpha_i^{\{i,j\}}, \beta_j^{\{i,j\}}) \in \Delta$. In a (minor) abuse of notation, the ordering of $i$ and $j$ in the superscript on $p$ will matter. The relative ask price of good $j$ and bid price of $i$ are represented as $p^{\{j,i\}} \equiv (\alpha_j^{\{i,j\}}, \beta_i^{\{i,j\}}) \in \Delta$. Thus there are two operative price 1-simplices at each trading post. The full price space then is $\Delta^{N(N-1)}$, the $N(N-1)$-fold Cartesian product of $\Delta$ with itself; its typical element is $p \in \Delta^{N(N-1)}$. Then the ask price of $i$ at $\{i,j\}$ in units of $j$ is $\frac{\alpha_i^{\{i,j\}}}{\beta_j^{\{i,j\}}}$ and the bid price of $i$ is $\frac{\beta_i^{\{i,j\}}}{\alpha_j^{\{i,j\}}}$. In the less general notation of Chapter 3, $q_i^{\{i,j\}} \equiv \frac{\beta_i^{\{i,j\}}}{\alpha_j^{\{i,j\}}}$, for $\alpha_j^{\{i,j\}} > 0$.

Prices can then be read as rates of exchange between goods, distinguishing between bid (selling or wholesale) prices and ask (buying or retail) prices. Thus the ask price of a steak dinner might be 20 chocolate bars and the bid price 15 chocolate bars. Note that the ask price of a chocolate bar then is the inverse of the bid price of a steak dinner. That is, the ask price of a chocolate bar is 0.067 steak dinner and the bid price of a chocolate bar is 0.05 steak dinner.

# 4 BUDGET CONSTRAINTS AND TRADING OPPORTUNITIES

The budget constraint is simply that at each pairwise trading post, at prevailing prices, in each transaction, payment is given for goods received. That is, at trading post $\{i, j\}$, an ask−bid price pair is quoted $p^{\{i,j\}} \equiv (\alpha_i^{\{i,j\}}, \beta_j^{\{i,j\}}) \in \Delta$ expressing the ask price of $i$ in terms of $j$ and a bid price of $j$ in terms of $i$. A firm or household's trading plans $(y, x) \in R^{2N(N-1)}$ specifies the following transactions at trading post $\{i, j\}$: $y_i^{\{i,j\}}$ (at ask prices − retail) in $i$, $y_j^{\{i,j\}}$ (at ask prices − retail) in $j$, $x_i^{\{i,j\}}$ (at bid prices − wholesale) in $i$, $x_j^{\{i,j\}}$ (at bid prices − wholesale) in $j$. Positive values of these transactions are purchases. Negative values are sales. At each trading post (of two goods) there are four quantities to specify in a trading plan. Then the budget constraint facing firms and households at each trading post is that value delivered must equal value received. That is:

$$0 = (\alpha_i^{\{i,j\}}, \beta_j^{\{i,j\}}) \cdot (y_i^{\{i,j\}}, x_j^{\{i,j\}}) , \, 0 = (\alpha_j^{\{i,j\}}, \beta_i^{\{i,j\}}) \cdot (y_j^{\{i,j\}}, x_i^{\{i,j\}}). \quad \textbf{(B)}$$

**(B)** says that purchases of $i$ at the bid price are repaid by sales of $j$ at the ask price, purchases of $i$ at the ask price are repaid by sales of $j$ at the bid price. **(B)** is the generalization to this model of firms and households of Chapter 3's trading post balance constraint (T.ii). For household $h$, purchases at ask prices in Chapter 3 were characterized as $b_i^{h\{i,j\}} \leq q_j^{\{i,j\}} \cdot s_j^{h\{i,j\}}$, where sales, $s_j^{h\{i,j\}} \geq 0$ were made at the bid price $q_j^{\{i,j\}}$. The treatment in this chapter uses a more general notation treating firms and households in common, where transactions at bid prices are denoted $x$ and at ask prices are denoted $y$. Households, unlike firms, are supposed always to buy at ask prices and sell at bid prices. For the households then, there is a simple concordance between the notations:

$$0 \geq x_j^{h\{i,j\}} \equiv -s_j^{h\{i,j\}},$$

$$0 \leq y_i^{h\{i,j\}} \equiv b_i^{h\{i,j\}}.$$

### 4.1    A Common Budget Constraint for Firms and Households

Given a price vector $p \in \Delta^{N(N-1)}$ the array of trades fulfilling (**B**) is the set of trades fulfilling the $N(N-1)$ local budget constraints at the trading-posts. Denote this set

$$\mathbf{M}(p) \equiv$$

$$\{(y, x) \in \mathbf{R}^{2N(N-1)} | (y, x) \text{ fulfills (\textbf{B}) at } p \text{ for all } i, j = 1, \ldots, N, i \neq j\}.$$

## 5    FIRMS

Firms perform the market-making function, incurring transaction costs. The population of firms is a finite set denoted $F$, with typical element $f \in F$. Thus, firm $f$'s technology set may specify that $f$'s purchase of inputs to the transaction process (perhaps at ask prices) in exchange for $i$ on the $\{i, input\}$ market and purchase of $i$ and $j$ wholesale on the $\{i, j\}$ market allows $f$ to sell $i$ and $j$ (retail) on the $\{i, j\}$ market. That is how $f$ can become a market maker. If there is a sufficient difference between bid and ask prices so that $f$ can cover the cost of its inputs with a surplus left over, that surplus becomes $f$'s profits, to be rebated to $f$'s shareholders.

### 5.1    Transaction and Production Technology

Firm $f$'s technology set is $Y^f$. We assume:

**P.0**    $Y^f \subset \mathbf{R}^{2N(N-1)}$.

The typical element of $Y^f$ is $(y^f, x^f)$, a pair of $N(N-1)$-dimensional vectors. The $N(N-1)$-dimensional vector $y^f$ represents $f$'s transactions at ask (retail) prices; the $N(N-1)$-dimensional vector $x^f$ represents $f$'s transactions at bid (wholesale) prices. The 2-dimensional vector $y^{f\{i,j\}}$ represents $f$'s transactions at ask (retail) prices at trading post $\{i, j\}$; the 2-dimensional vector $x^{f\{i,j\}}$ represents $f$'s transactions at bid (wholesale) prices at trading post $\{i, j\}$. The typical coordinates $y_i^{f\{i,j\}}, x_i^{f\{i,j\}}$ are $f$'s action with respect to good $i$ at the $\{i, j\}$ trading post. Since $f$ may act as a wholesaler/retailer/market maker, entries anywhere in $(y^{f\{i,j\}}, x^{f\{i,j\}})$ may be positive or negative — subject of course to constraints of technology $Y^f$ and prices $\mathbf{M}(p)$. This distinguishes the firm from the typical household. The typical household can only sell at bid prices and buy at ask prices.

The entry $y_i^{f\{i,j\}}$, represents $f$'s actions at ask prices with regard to good

$i$ at trading post $\{i, j\}$. $y_i^{f\{i,j\}} > 0$ represents a purchase of $i$ at the $\{i, j\}$ trading post (at the ask price). $y_i^{f\{i,j\}} < 0$ represents a sale of $i$ at the ask price.

The entry $x_i^{f\{i,j\}}$, represents $f$'s actions at bid prices with regard to good $i$ at trading post $\{i, j\}$. $x_i^{f\{i,j\}} > 0$ represents a purchase of $i$ at the trading post (at the bid price). $x_i^{f\{i,j\}} < 0$ represents a sale of $i$ at the bid price.

A firm with three elements, the technical capability to buy at the bid price and to sell at the ask price and a sufficiently efficient transactions technology, may become a market maker. A firm that is an active market maker at $\{i, j\}$, will typically buy at the bid price and sell at the ask price. A firm that is not a market maker may sell at the bid price and buy at the ask price.

In addition to indicating the transaction possibilities, $Y^f$ includes the usual production possibilities. The usual assumptions on production technology apply. For each $f \in F$, assume:

**P.I**   $Y^f$ is convex.
**P.II**   $0 \in Y^f$, where 0 indicates the zero vector in $\mathbf{R}^{2N(N-1)}$.
**P.III**   $Y^f$ is closed.

The aggregate technology set is the sum of individual firm technology sets. $Y \equiv \Sigma_{f \in F} Y^f$. It fulfills the familiar *no free lunch* and *irreversibility* conditions.

**P.IV**   [(a)] if $(y, x) \in Y$ and $(y, x) \neq 0$, then $y_i^{\{i,j\}} + x_i^{\{i,j\}} > 0$ for some $i, j$.

[(b)] if $(y, x) \in Y$ and $(y, x) \neq 0$, then $-(y, x) \notin Y$.

Denote the initial resource endowment of the economy as $r \in \mathbf{R}_+^N$. Then we define the attainable production plans of the economy as:

$$\hat{Y} \equiv \left\{ (y, x) \in Y | r_i \geq \sum_j (y_i^{\{i,j\}} + x_i^{\{i,j\}}) \text{ all } i = 1, 2, \ldots, N \right\}.$$

Attainable production plans for firm $f$ can then be described as:

$$\hat{Y}^f \equiv \{ (y^f, x^f) \in Y^f | \text{ there is } (y^k, x^k) \in Y^k \text{ for each } k \in F, k \neq f, \text{ so that}$$

$$\left[ \sum_{k \in F, k \neq f} (y^k, x^k) + (y^f, x^f) \right] \in \hat{Y} \}.$$

**Lemma 11.1**   Assume P.0−P.IV. Then $\hat{Y}$ and $\hat{Y}^f$ are closed, convex, and bounded.

**Proof**   Starr (1997, Theorems 8.1, 8.2). QED

## 5.2   Firm Maximand and Transactions Function

The firm formulates a production plan and a trading plan. The firm's opportunity set for net yields after transactions fulfilling budget is $E^f(p) \equiv [\mathbf{M}(p) - Y^f] \cap \mathbf{R}_+^{2N(N-1)}$. That is, consider the firm's production, purchase, and sale possibilities, net after paying for them, and what is left is the net yield. Using the sign conventions we have adopted − purchases are positive coordinates, sales are negative coordinates − the net yield is then the negative coordinates (supplies) in a trading plan that are not absorbed by payments due and the net purchases not required as inputs to the firm. The supplies are subtracted out, so the surpluses enter $E^f(p)$ as positive coordinates.

A typical element of these surplus supplies is denoted $(y', x') \in E^f(p)$. In this notation $y'$ and $x'$ are dummies, not actual marketed supplies and demands.

Now consider $(y', x') \in E^f(p)$. In each good $i$, the net surplus available in good $i$ is $w_i^f \equiv \Sigma_{j=1}^{N} (y_i'^{\{i,j\}} + x_i'^{\{i,j\}})$ and firm $f$'s surplus is the vector $w^f$ of these coordinates. To give this notion a functional notation, let $W(y', x') \equiv w^f$ described here.

There are $N - 1$ trading posts where each good $i$ is traded, at $N - 1$ rates of exchange. The notion of 'profit' is not well defined. In the absence of a single family of well-defined prices, it is difficult to characterize optimizing behavior for the firm. *Faute de mieux* we shall give the firm a scalar maximand with argument $p, y', x'$. Firm $f$ is assumed to have a real-valued, continuous maximand $v^f(p; y', x')$. We take $v^f$ to be monotone and concave in $(y', x')$. This description of $v^f$ includes as a special case the usual firm profit function (when $p$ is sufficiently uniform across trading posts that the usual notion of profit is well defined).

The firm's optimizing choice (which may not be well defined) then is:

$$G^f(p) \equiv \{\operatorname{argmax} v^f(p; y', x') \in E^f(p)\}.$$

This results in the firm's market behavior (without any constraint requiring actions to stay in a bounded range) described by:

$$H^f(p) \equiv \{(y, x) \in \mathbf{M}(p) | [(y, x) + (y', x')] \in Y^f, (y', x') \in G^f(p)\}.$$

This marketed plan then results in the market and dividend plan:

$$S^f(p) \equiv \{(y, x; w) | (y, x) \in H^f(p), [(y, x) + (y', x')] \in Y^f,$$

$$(y', x') \in G^f(p); w = W(y', x')\}.$$

The logic of this definition is that $(y', x') \geq 0$ is the surplus left over after the firm $f$ has performed according to its technology and subject to prevailing prices.

It is possible that $S^f(p)$ is not well defined, since the opportunity set may be unbounded. In the light of Lemma 11.1, there is a constant $c > 0$ sufficiently large so that for all $f \in F$, $\hat{Y}^f$ is strictly contained in a closed ball, denoted $B_c$ of radius $c$ centered at the origin of $R^{2N(N-1)}$. Following the technique of Arrow and Debreu (1954), constrained market behavior for the firm will consist of limiting its production choices to $Y^f \cap B_c$. This leads to the constrained surplus:

$$\widetilde{E}^f(p) \equiv [[\mathbf{M}(p) \cap B_c] - [Y^f \cap B_c]] \cap \mathbf{R}_+^{2N(N-1)}.$$

$$\widetilde{G}^f(p) \equiv \{\text{argmax } v^f(p; y', x') \in \widetilde{E}^f(p)\}.$$

$$\widetilde{H}^f(p) \equiv \{(y, x) \in \mathbf{M}(p) | [(y, x) + (y', x')] \in Y^f \cap B_c, (y', x') \in \widetilde{G}^f(p)\}.$$

The firm's constrained (to $B_c$) market behavior then is defined as:

$$\widetilde{S}^f(p) \equiv \{(y, x; w) | (y, x) \in \widetilde{H}^f(p),$$

$$[(y, x) + (y', x')] \in Y^f \cap B_c, (y', x') \in \widetilde{G}^f(p); w = W(y', x')\}.$$

**Lemma 11.2** Assume P.0−P.IV. Then $\widetilde{E}^f(p)$ is convex valued, nonempty, upper and lower hemicontinuous.

**Proof** Upper hemicontinuity and convexity follow from closedness and convexity of the underlying sets. $0 \in \widetilde{E}^f(p)$ always, so nonemptiness is fulfilled. Lower hemicontinuity requires some work.

Let $p^v \to p^o$, $(y^o, x^o) \in \widetilde{E}^f(p^o)$. We seek $(y^v, x^v) \in \widetilde{E}^f(p^v)$ so that $(y^v, x^v) \to (y^o, x^o)$. If $(y^o, x^o) = 0$, existence of $(y^v, x^v) \to (y^o, x^o)$ is trivially satisfied. Suppose instead $(y^o, x^o) \geq 0$ (the inequality applies coordinatewise). Then in an $\varepsilon$-neighborhood of $(y^o, x^o)$, for $v$ sufficiently large, we seek to show that there is $(y^v, x^v) \in \widetilde{E}(p^v)$. $(y^v, x^v)$ is the required sequence. To demonstrate this, note that $\widetilde{E}(p^v)$ is defined as the intersection of a convex-valued correspondence lower hemicontinuous in $p$ with a constant convex set. When $(y^o, x^o) \geq 0$ and $(y^o, x^o) \in \widetilde{E}^f(p^o)$ it follows that the relative interior of $\widetilde{E}^f(p^o)$ is nonempty. It is sufficient then to apply Green and Heller (1981, p. 48, 8, lower).[4] QED

**Lemma 11.3**   Assume P.0−P.IV. Then $\widetilde{G}^f(p), \widetilde{H}^f(p), \widetilde{S}^f(p)$ are well defined, nonempty, upper hemicontinuous, and convex valued for all $p \in \Delta^{N(N-1)}$.

**Proof**   Note compactness of $B_c$. Apply theorem of the maximum, continuity and concavity of $v^f$. QED

**Lemma 11.4**   Assume P.0−P.IV. Let $[\widetilde{G}^f(p) + \widetilde{H}^f(p)] \cap \hat{Y}^f \neq \varnothing$. Then $[\widetilde{G}^f(p) + \widetilde{H}^f(p)] \subseteq [G^f(p) + H^f(p)]$.

**Proof**   Recall that $B_c$ strictly includes $\hat{Y}^f$. Then the result follows from convexity of $Y^f$ and $\hat{Y}^f$ and concavity of $v^f(p; y', x')$. The proof follows the model of Starr (1997, Theorem 8.3). Let $(y^{*\prime}, x^{*\prime}) \in \widetilde{G}^f(p), (y^*, x^*) \in \widetilde{H}^f(p), [(y^{*\prime}, x^{*\prime}) + (y^*, x^*)] \in \hat{Y}^f \subset B_c$. Use a proof by contradiction. Suppose not. Then there is $(y, x) \in Y^f$ so that $(y, x) - (y^o, x^o) = (y', x')$, where $v^f(p; y', x') > v^f(p; y^{*\prime}, x^{*\prime})$, $(y', x') \in E^f(p)$, and $(y^o, x^o) \in M(p)$. But convexity of $Y^f$ and concavity of $v^f$ imply that on the chord between $(y^*, x^*)$ and $(y, x)$ there is $[\widetilde{\alpha}(y^*, x^*) + (1 - \widetilde{\alpha})(y, x)] \in B_c$ for $1 \geq \widetilde{\alpha} > 0$ where $v^f(p; [\widetilde{\alpha}(y^{*\prime}, x^{*\prime}) + (1 - \widetilde{\alpha})(y', x')]) > v^f(p; y^{*\prime}, x^{*\prime})$. This is a contradiction. QED

### 5.3   Inclusion of Constrained Supply in Unconstrained Supply

$(y, x; w) \in \widetilde{S}^f(p)$ implies $(y, x) \in B_c$, a bounded set. $w \in \mathbf{R}_+^N$ is $f$'s profits. By construction there is $K > 0$ so that $w$ is contained in the nonnegative quadrant of a ball of radius $K$ centered at the origin, denoted $B_K \subset \mathbf{R}_+^N$.

**Lemma 11.5**   Let $p \in \Delta^{N(N-1)}$ such that $\widetilde{S}^f(p) \cap [\hat{Y}^f \times B_K] \neq \varnothing$. Then $S^f(p)$ is well defined and nonempty. Further $\widetilde{S}^f(p) \subseteq S^f(p)$.

**Proof**   Lemma 11.4. QED

## 6   HOUSEHOLDS

There is a finite set of households, $H$, with typical element $h$.

### 6.1   Endowment and Consumption Set

$h \in H$ has a possible consumption set, taken for simplicity to be the nonnegative quadrant of $\mathbf{R}^N$, $\mathbf{R}_+^N$. $h \in H$ is endowed with $r^h \gg 0$ assumed to be strictly positive to avoid boundary problems. $h \in H$ has a share $\eta^{hf} \geq 0$ of firm $f$, so that $\Sigma_{h \in H} \eta^{hf} = 1$.

## 6.2 Trades and Payment Constraint

$h \in H$ chooses $(y^h, x^h) \in \mathbf{R}^{2N(N-1)}$ subject to the following restrictions. A household always balances its budget, sells wholesale and buys retail:

$$0 \geq x_i^{h\{i,j\}} \text{ for all } i, j. \tag{11.1}$$

$$y_i^{h\{i,j\}} \geq 0 \text{ for all } i, j. \tag{11.2}$$

$$(y^h, x^h) \in \mathbf{M}(p). \tag{11.3}$$

## 6.3 Maximand and Demand

Household $h$'s share of profits from firm $f$ is part of $h$'s endowment and enters directly into consumption. When the profits of all firms $f \in F$, $w^f$ in $(y^f, x^f; w^f)$, are well defined, $f$ distributes to shareholders $w^f$, and $h$'s consumption of good $i$ is:

$$c_i^h \equiv r_i^h + \left[ \sum_{f \in F} \eta^{hf} w^f \right]_i + \sum_{j=1}^{N} x_i^{h\{i,j\}} + \sum_{j=1}^{N} y_i^{h\{i,j\}}. \tag{11.4'}$$

However, prices $p$ may be such that $S^f(p)$ is not well defined for some $f$. Then we may wish to discuss the constrained version of (11.4), where $\widetilde{w}^f$ comes from $(y^f, x^f; \widetilde{w}^f) \in \widetilde{S}^f(p)$.

$$c_i^h \equiv r_i^h + \left[ \sum_{f \in F} \eta^{hf} \widetilde{w}^f \right]_i + \sum_{j=1}^{N} x_i^{h\{i,j\}} + \sum_{j=1}^{N} y_i^{h\{i,j\}}. \tag{11.4}$$

In addition, $h$'s consumption must be nonnegative:

$$c^h \geq 0. \text{ The inequality applies coordinatewise.} \tag{11.5}$$

**C.I** For all $h \in H$, $h$'s maximand is the continuous, quasi-concave, real-valued, strictly monotone, utility function $u^h(c^h)$. $u^h : \mathbf{R}_+^N \to \mathbf{R}$.

$h$'s planned transactions function is defined as $D^h : \Delta^{N(N-1)} \times \mathbf{R}^{N\#F} \to \mathbf{R}^{2N(N-1)}$. Let $w$ denote $(w^1, w^2, w^3, \ldots, w^f, \ldots, w^{\#F})$.

$D^h(p, w) \equiv \{ (y^h, x^h) \in \mathbf{R}^{2N(N-1)} | (y^h, x^h)$ maximizes $u^h(c^h)$, subject to (11.1)–(11.5)} However, $D^h(p, w)$ may not be well defined when opportunity sets are unbounded (when ask prices of some goods are zero) and $w$ may not be well defined for $p$ such that $S^f(p)$ is not well defined for some $f$. To treat this issue, let $B_K^{\#F}$ be the #$F$-fold Cartesian product of $B_K$, and define $\widetilde{D}^h : \Delta^{N(N-1)} \times B_K^{\#F} \to B_c$.

$\widetilde{D}^h(p, w) \equiv \{ (y^h, x^h) | (y^h, x^h)$ maximizes $u^h(c^h)$, subject to (11.1)–(11.3), (11.4'), (11.5) and $(y^h, x^h) \in B_c \}$. The restriction to $B_c$ in this definition assures that $\widetilde{D}^h(p)$ represents the result of optimization on a bounded set, and is well defined.

**Lemma 11.6** Assume P.0 − P.IV, C.I. Then $\widetilde{D}^h(p,w)$ is nonempty, upper hemicontinuous and convex valued, for all $p \in \Delta^{N(N-1)}$, $w \in B_K^{\#F}$. The range of $\widetilde{D}^h(p, w)$ is compact. For $(p, w)$ such that $|(y^h, x^h)| < c$ for (some) $(y^h, x^h) \in \widetilde{D}^h(p, w)$, it follows that $\widetilde{D}^h(p, w) \subseteq D^h(p, w)$.

**Proof** (Note to the reader: this proof includes an unfortunate confusion of notation. $c$ without superscript denotes a large real number indicating the radius of $B_c$, a ball strictly containing all attainable transactions of the typical firm. $c^h$ and $c*$ (with superscript) denote consumption vectors.) Apply theorem of the maximum, noting continuity and quasi-concavity of $u^h$, convexity of constraint sets defined by (11.1)−(11.5) or by (11.1)−(11.3), (11.4′), and (11.5). Inclusion of $\widetilde{D}^h(p, w)$ in $D^h(p, w)$ follows the pattern of Starr (1997, Theorem 9.1(b)). Proof by contradiction. Suppose not. Then there is $(y*, x*) \in D^h(p, w)$ with associated $c*$ so that $u^h(c*) > u^h(c^h)$. But recall $|(y^h, x^h)| < c$. On the chord between $(y^h, x^h)$ and $(y*, x*)$ there is $[\widetilde{\alpha}(y*,x*) + (1 - \widetilde{\alpha})(y^h, x^h)], 1 > \widetilde{\alpha} > 0$, fulfilling (11.1)−(11.3), (11.4′), (11.5), and $|[\widetilde{\alpha}(y*,x*) + (1 - \widetilde{\alpha})(y^h, x^h)]| = c$ so that $u(\widetilde{\alpha}c* + (1 - \widetilde{\alpha})c^h) > u(c^h)$. This is a contradiction. QED

## 7 EXCESS DEMAND

Let $(p, w') \in \Delta^{N(N-1)} \times B_K^{\#F}$. Constrained excess demand and dividends at $(p, w')$ is defined as:

$$\widetilde{Z}: \Delta^{N(N-1)} \times B_K^{\#F} \to \mathbf{R}^{2N(N-1)} \times B_K^{\#F}.$$

$$\widetilde{Z}(p, w') \equiv$$

$$\left\{ \left( \sum_{f \in F} (y^f, x^f) + \sum_{h \in H} \widetilde{D}^h(p, w'), w^1, w^2, \ldots, w^f, \ldots, w^{\#F} \right) \middle| (y^f, x^f, w^f) \in \widetilde{S}^f(p) \right\}.$$

**Lemma 11.7** Assume P.0−P.IV, and C.I. The range of $\widetilde{Z}$ is bounded. $\widetilde{Z}$ is upper hemicontinuous and convex valued for all $(p, w') \in \Delta^{N(N-1)} \times B_K^{\#F}$.

**Lemma 11.8** (Walras's Law) Let $(p, w') \in \Delta^{N(N-1)} \times B_K^{\#F}$. Let $(y, x, w) \in \widetilde{Z}(p, w')$. Then for each $i, j = 1, \ldots, N, i \neq j$, we have:

$$0 = (\alpha_i^{\{i,j\}}, \beta_j^{\{i,j\}}) \cdot (y_i^{\{i,j\}}, x_j^{\{i,j\}}), \, 0 = (\alpha_j^{\{i,j\}}, \beta_i^{\{i,j\}}) \cdot (y_j^{\{i,j\}}, x_i^{\{i,j\}}). \quad \textbf{(W)}$$

**Proof** The element $(y, x)$ of $(y, x, w) \in \widetilde{Z}(p, w')$ is the sum of elements $(y^f, x^f)$ of $\widetilde{S}^f(p)$ and $(y^h, x^h)$ of $\widetilde{D}^h(p, w')$ each of which is subject to **(B)**. QED

## 8 EQUILIBRIUM

Let $\Xi$ denote a compact convex subset of $R^{2N(N-1)}$ so that $\Xi \times B_K^{\#F}$ includes the range of $\widetilde{Z}$. Let $z \in \Xi$, $z \equiv ((y_1^{\{1,2\}}, x_2^{\{1,2\}}), \ldots, (y_i^{\{i,j\}}, x_j^{\{i,j\}}), \ldots, (y_{N-1}^{\{N-1,N\}}, x_N^{\{N-1,N\}}))$. Define $\rho: \Xi \to \Delta^{N(N-1)}$

$\rho(z) \equiv \{p^o \in \Delta^{N(N-1)} |$ For each $i, j = 1, 2, \ldots, N, i \neq j, p^{o\{i,j\}} \in \Delta$ maximizes $p^{\{i,j\}} \cdot (y_i^{\{i,j\}}, x_j^{\{i,j\}})$ subject to $p^{\{i,j\}} \in \Delta\}$.

**Lemma 11.9** $\rho$ is upper hemicontinuous and convex valued for all $z \in \Xi$.

Define $\Gamma: \Delta^{N(N-1)} \times \Xi \times B_K^{\#F} \to \Delta^{N(N-1)} \times \Xi \times B_K^{\#F}$.
$\Gamma(p, z, w') \equiv \rho(z) \times \widetilde{Z}(p, w')$.

**Lemma 11.10** Assume P.0−P.IV, and C.I. Then $\Gamma$ is upper hemicontinuous and convex valued on $\Delta^{N(N-1)} \times \Xi \times B_K^{\#F}$. $\Gamma$ has a fixed point $(p^*, z^*, w^*)$ and $0 = z^*$.

**Proof** Upper hemicontinuity and convexity are established in Lemmas 11.7 and 11.9. Existence of the fixed point $(p^*, z^*)$ then follows from the Kakutani fixed point theorem. To demonstrate that $z^* = 0$, note Lemma 11.8 and strict monotonicity of $u^h$. QED

Definition: $(p^*, w^*) \in \Delta^{N(N-1)} \times B_K^{\#F}$ is said to be an equilibrium if:

$(0, w^*) \in$

$$\left\{ \left( \sum_{f \in F} (y^f, x^f) + \sum_{h \in H} D^h(p^*, w^*), w^1, w^2, \ldots, w^f, \ldots, w^{\#F} \right) | (y^f, x^f, w^f) \in S^f(p^*) \right\}$$

where 0 is the origin in $\mathbf{R}^{2N(N-1)}$.

**Theorem 11.1** Assume P.0−P.IV, C.I. Then there is an equilibrium $(p^*, w^*) \in \Delta^{N(N-1)} \times B_K^{\#F}$.

**Proof** Apply Lemmas 11.5, 11.6, 11.10. Lemma 11.10 provides $(p^*, z^*, w^*) \in \Delta^{N(N-1)} \times \Xi \times B_K^{\#F}$ so that $0 = z^*$, where:

$$(z^*, w^*) \in \{ (\Sigma_{f \in F}(y^f, x^f) + \Sigma_{h \in H} \widetilde{D}^h(p^*, w^*), w^1, w^2, \ldots, w^f, \ldots, w^{\#F}) |$$

$$(y^f, x^f, w^f) \in \widetilde{S}^f(p^*) \}.$$

Then $\widetilde{S^f}(p^*) \cap [\hat{Y}^f \times B_K] \neq \emptyset$, so by Lemma 11.5, $\widetilde{S^f}(p^*) \subseteq S^f(p^*).0 = z^*$, implies that $|(y^{*h}, x^{*h})| < c$, so by lemma 11.6, $\tilde{D}^h(p^*, w^*) \subseteq D^h(p^*, w^*)$. But then $(0, w^*) \in \{(\Sigma_{f \in F}(y^f, x^f) + \Sigma_{h \in H}D^h(p^*, w^*), \quad w^1, w^2, \ldots, w^f, \ldots, w^{\#F})| (y^f, x^f, w^f) \in S^f(p^*)\}$. Then $(p^*, w^*)$ is an equilibrium. QED

# 9  MEDIA OF EXCHANGE, COMMODITY MONEYS

Let $(y^h, x^h) \in D^h(p, w')$ be household $h$'s $2N(N - 1)$-dimensional transaction vector. The $x$ coordinates are typically sales (negative sign) at bid prices; the $y$ coordinates are typically purchases (positive sign) at ask prices. Then we can characterize $h$'s gross transactions in good $i$ as:

$$\sum_j y_i^{h\{i,j\}} - \sum_j x_i^{h\{i,j\}} \equiv \gamma_i^h.$$

Further, the absolute value of $h$'s net transactions in good $i$, is:

$$|\sum_j y_i^{h\{i,j\}} + \sum_j x_i^{h\{i,j\}}| \equiv v_i^h.$$

The $N$-dimensional vector $\gamma^h$ with typical element $\gamma_i^h$ is $h$'s gross trade. The $N$-dimensional vector $v^h$ with typical element $v_i^h$ is $h$'s net trade vector (in absolute value). $\mu^h \equiv \gamma^h - v^h$ is $h$'s flow of goods as media of exchange, gross trades minus net trades.

Since firms perform a market-making function, buying and selling the same good at a single trading post, a more complex view of their transactions is needed to sort out trading flows used as media of exchange. In particular, for firms, we should net out offsetting transactions within a single trading post. Thus for $f \in F$, $f$'s gross transactions in $i$, netting out intra-post transactions is:

$$\sum_j |[y_i^{f\{i,j\}} + x_i^{f\{i,j\}}]| \equiv \gamma_i^f.$$

The corresponding net transaction is:

$$|\sum_j [y_i^{f\{i,j\}} + x_i^{f\{i,j\}}]| \equiv v_i^f.$$

The $N$-dimensional vector $\gamma^f$ with typical element $\gamma_i^f$ is $f$'s gross inter-post trade. The $N$-dimensional vector $v^f$ with typical element $v_i^f$ is $h$'s net inter-post trade vector (in absolute value). $\mu^f \equiv \gamma^f - v^f$ is $f$'s flow of goods as media of exchange, gross (inter-post) trades minus net trades.

The total ($N$-dimensional vector) flow of media of exchange among households and firms is then $\Sigma_{h \in H}\mu^h + \Sigma_{f \in F}\mu^f$. This expression,

$$\sum_{h \in H} \mu^h + \sum_{f \in F} \mu^f$$

is the flow of commodity moneys.

## 10   CONCLUSION

The trading post equilibrium establishes a well-defined demand for media of exchange as an outcome of the market equilibrium. Media of exchange (commodity moneys) are characterized as goods flows acting as the carrier of value between transactions (not fulfilling final demands or input requirements themselves), the difference between gross and net trades.

This chapter creates a parsimonious model where a medium of exchange (commodity money) is an outcome of the (slightly augmented) Arrow–Debreu general equilibrium. The monetary structure of trade is a result of the price theory general equilibrium. Monetary trade is not a separate assumption; monetary exchange is an outcome, a direct implication of the general equilibrium when there are multiple distinct budget constraints facing each agent.

The trades of firms and households in a trading post economy may be characterized by many separate transactions, each fulfilling a separate budget constraint. In an economy of $N$ commodities there are $\frac{1}{2}N(N-1)$ trading posts, one for each pair of goods. The trading post model reformulates the budget so that each of many separate transactions fulfills its own budget constraint. This treatment generates a demand for carriers of value (media of exchange) moving among successive trades. Virtually the same axiomatic structure (Arrow and Debreu, 1954) that ensures the existence of general equilibrium in the model of a unified market without transaction costs yields existence of equilibrium and a well-defined demand for media of exchange in this disaggregated setting.

## NOTES

1. This chapter follows the modeling approach of Starr (2008b).
2. Consistent with Occam's razor.
3. Nevertheless, the examples are intended to be robust. The parametric examples should be contained in an open subset of parameter space where the results of the example remain valid.
4. 'If  $\gamma_i, i = 1, 2,$  are two l.h.c. convex-valued correspondences such that $int\gamma_1(x^o) \cap int\gamma_2(x^o) \neq \varnothing$, then $\gamma_1 \cap \gamma_2$ is l.h.c. at $x^o$.'

# 12.   Efficiency of commodity money equilibrium[1]

In an Arrow–Debreu model all competitive equilibrium allocations are Pareto efficient; that is the first fundamental theorem of economics. That result does not fully generalize to the trading post model with transaction costs. The efficiency concept must be suitably refined to reflect the technically necessary transaction costs associated with reallocating ownership from producers and suppliers to consumers. Those transaction costs are technically necessary and do not interfere with efficient resource allocation. When the multiplicity of budget constraints results in a reallocation of resources or incurring additional transaction costs to fulfill them, the resulting reallocation is a resource cost needed to fulfill the administrative constraint of budget balance rather than technical necessity. Those costs are wasted and the resulting allocation cannot be Pareto efficient. Conversely when there is a transaction-costless medium of exchange, the resulting trading post equilibrium allocation is Pareto efficient.

## 1   TRANSACTION COSTS, ESSENTIAL AND INESSENTIAL SEQUENCE ECONOMIES

The issues of general equilibrium with transaction cost, efficiency of allocation and the implications for the role of money appear in Foley (1970), Hahn (1971, 1973), and Starrett (1973). Foley considers a static equilibrium with (consistent with the Arrow–Debreu treatment) a single market meeting. All of the formal structure of the Arrow–Debreu economy is maintained while the transaction process is treated as a production activity. Each of $N$ goods has a bid and ask (wholesale and retail) price with the resulting dimensionality of the price space at $2N$. As in Debreu (1959) the count $N$ includes futures markets for all of the relevant goods. Foley's distinctive powerful insight is that this structure is mathematically equivalent to the Arrow–Debreu model. Assuming the usual continuity and convexity assumptions, a competitive equilibrium exists in the convex transaction cost economy, and the resulting allocation is Pareto efficient. The notion of Pareto efficiency here needs to take account of transaction costs: moving ownership from one firm or household to another is a resource-using activity. Efficiency consists of efficient allocation net of the necessary resource cost of reassigning ownership.

Hahn (1973) treats the reopening of markets over time in a sequence economy. Markets reopen over time (unlike the Arrow–Debreu model) and a budget constraint is enforced at each date. The treatment distinguishes between *essential* and *inessential* sequence economies. The issue treated is whether two otherwise identical economies have significantly different equilibrium prices and resource allocation depending on the character of the budget constraint: a single Arrow–Debreu budget for each household versus a time-dated sequence of budget constraints in a sequence economy. In this comparison it is necessary to take account of transaction costs, so the reference point is not the conventional Arrow–Debreu equilibrium without transaction costs (Debreu, 1959). Rather, it is the allocation in an Arrow–Debreu economy with transaction costs (Foley, 1970).

This chapter adopts the same usage. The efficiency concept is subject to technically necessary transaction costs. A trading post equilibrium is 'inessential' if the resulting allocation is Walrasian, the same as in an Arrow–Debreu (Foley) economy with transaction costs. The equilibrium is inessential if the multi-faceted structure of the trading post budget constraint has no effect in itself on the resulting allocation of resources. Conversely, the trading post equilibrium will be described as 'essential' if the equilibrium resource allocation is non-Walrasian, differing because of the structure of budget constraints.

Then the resource allocation in an inessential trading post economy is a Walrasian equilibrium allocation and it is Pareto efficient by the first fundamental theorem of welfare economics. Conversely, a trading post economy is essential when the multi-faceted structure of budget constraints renders the equilibrium allocation of resources different from an Arrow–Debreu equilibrium (taking full account of the effect of transaction costs, with a complete array of futures markets). Then the equilibrium allocation will not be a Walrasian equilibrium and may be Pareto inefficient. The inefficiency arises in either of two ways: additional resources may be expended in fulfillment of the multiplicity of budget constraints, or the allocation may be shifted (relative to Walrasian equilibrium) to fulfill the additional constraints. Since these circumstances represent real resource allocations to fulfill a purely administrative constraint, the reallocation is regarded as Pareto inefficient. This treatment is similar to Hahn (1973)'s treatment of sequence economies. A full development of efficiency conditions and detailed characterization of (in)essentiality is a significant topic, beyond the scope of this volume.

The array of economies subject to general equilibrium modeling includes essential and inessential trading post economies with resultant Walrasian and non-Walrasian allocations. Since the designation 'essential' or 'inessential' is based on the character of endogenous equilibrium pricing, it seems problematic to distinguish essential from inessential trading post economies a priori. The alternative is to review examples, several of which are presented below.

## 2   ECONOMIES ACTIVELY USING MEDIA OF EXCHANGE

The examples of sections 3.1 and 4.1 below illustrate the notion of trading post economies using media of exchange in equilibrium. They are characterized by economies where trade is mutually advantageous but direct trade between suppliers and final demanders at trading posts may be more costly in resources than indirect trade through a lower transaction cost instrument. This typically reflects two elements of the example: direct exchange is not fully mutually satisfactory because of absence of double coincidence of wants; and transaction costs in some commodity may be lower than others, favoring its use as a carrier of value in exchange. It is difficult fully to characterize the attributes of an economy, a priori, that will lead to these conditions, hence the reliance on examples. Nevertheless, the examples are intended to be robust. The parameters of the examples are intended to be elements of an open subset of parameter space where similar results hold.

## 3   PARETO EFFICIENCY OF TRADING POST EQUILIBRIUM WITH TRANSACTION COSTLESS MEDIA OF EXCHANGE

When there is a generally available zero-transaction cost medium of exchange, the trading post equilibrium will be inessential and the resulting allocation of resources Pareto efficient (taking into account transaction costs) (Hahn, 1973; Starrett, 1973). The allocation will be a Walrasian equilibrium. Supposing that the transaction costs of media of exchange in advanced monetary economies are low (if not nil), the zero-cost case should be a significant limiting case.

However important, the result is not new. The presence of a costless medium of exchange means that price ratios in a trading post economy will be the same as those of the corresponding Arrow−Debreu economy.

The example of Section 3.1 below illustrates the efficiency. The point of comparison is an economy with transaction costs, complete markets, efficient allocation in general equilibrium, a single budget constraint for each household and well-defined profit maximand for each firm, as in Foley (1970). Then apply the first fundamental theorem of welfare economics.

### 3.1 Example: A Natural Money absent Double Coincidence of Wants; Pareto-efficient Allocation in Trading Post Equilibrium

Let $H \equiv \{h = 1, 2, \ldots, N\}$ where $r_h^h = 100$ and where $u^h(c^h) = 20c_{h+1}^h + \Sigma_{n \neq h+1, n=1}^N c_n^h$ for $h = 1, \ldots, 99$, and for $h = N$, $u^h(c^h) = 20c_1^h + \Sigma_{n \neq 1, n=2}^N c_n^h$. There are $N$ households named $h = 1, 2, \ldots, N$; each endowed with 100 units of good $h$ and strongly preferring good $h + 1$ (mod $N$) to all others.

There are $\frac{1}{2}N(N-1)$ firms denoted $\{i, j\}, j > i, i, j = 1, 2, \ldots, N$. The transaction technology of $\{i, j\}, i \neq 1$ is $Y^{\{i,j\}} \equiv \{(y, x) | \text{for } k = i, j, 0 \geq y_k \geq -0.8x_k; \text{for } k \neq i, j, y_k = x_k = 0\}$. For $\{i, j\}, i = 1$, $Y^{\{i,j\}} \equiv \{(y, x) | \text{for } k = 1, y_1 = -x_1, \text{for } j \neq 1, 0 \geq y_j \geq -0.8x_j; \text{for } k \neq i, j, y_k = x_k = 0\}$. That is, for each pair of goods there is a distinct trading post firm $\{i, j\}$ and there is no arbitrage by firms between posts. Trade in all goods except good 1 experiences a 20 percent loss in the trading process.

To represent prices, we shall use the pricing notation of Chapter 11. The resulting equilibrium prices, for

$$i, j \neq 1 \text{ are } (\alpha_i^{\{i,j\}}, \beta_j^{\{i,j\}}) = \left(\frac{5}{8}, \frac{3}{8}\right).$$

For $i = 1, j \neq 2$ we have, $(\alpha_1^{\{1,j\}}, \beta_j^{\{1,j\}}) = \left(\frac{1}{2}, \frac{1}{2}\right)$, $(\alpha_j^{\{1,j\}}, \beta_1^{\{1,j\}}) = \left(\frac{5}{9}, \frac{4}{9}\right)$.

For $\{1, 2\}$ we have $(\alpha_1^{\{1,2\}}, \beta_2^{\{1,2\}}) = \left(\frac{1}{2}, \frac{1}{2}\right)$, $(\alpha_2^{\{1,2\}}, \beta_1^{\{1,2\}}) = \left(\frac{5}{9}, \frac{4}{9}\right)$.

The trade flows for

$$h = 2, 3, \ldots, N - 1, \text{ are } (x_h^{h\{h,1\}}, y_1^{h\{h,1\}}) = (-1, 1),$$

$$(x_1^{h\{1,h+1\}}, y_{h+1}^{h\{1,h+1\}}) = (-1, 0.8).$$

For $h = N$, $(x_N^{N\{1,N\}}, y_1^{N\{1,N\}}) = (-1, 0.8)$.

For $h = 1$, $(x_1^{1\{1,2\}}, y_2^{1\{1,2\}}) = (-1, 0.8)$. That is, direct trade of most goods $i$ for $j$ is prohibitively expensive, losing 40 percent of the goods in the transaction process. Indirect trade, through good 1, is more attractive since good 1 itself is transaction costless. The typical pattern of trade then is that household $h$ sells endowment, good $h$, for good 1, then sells good 1 for the desired good, $h + 1$. In the process, only 20 percent of goods are lost to transaction costs.

In this example all trade goes through good 1, and for $N - 1$ of $N$ traders good 1 is a medium of exchange. The allocation is Pareto efficient. How can it be Pareto efficient when 20 percent of goods are lost to transaction costs? Those costs were incurred in the necessary transfer of ownership to households that really desired the goods for consumption. Those costs, however regrettable, were technically necessary to the reallocation of consumption to those who could benefit from it. Hence Pareto efficiency.

Is the trading post equilibrium a Walrasian equilibrium? Individual agent trading behavior in the trading post model differs from Walrasian behavior (for example, in Foley, 1970) since it includes active use of a medium of exchange, good 1. But those trades are costless and net out to zero. The resulting resource allocation is fully consistent with Walrasian equilibrium and in a Foley economy (Arrow–Debreu with transaction costs) the allocation could be supported by Walrasian equilibrium prices. The allocation is Pareto efficient. This trading post economy is inessential.

## 4   PARETO INEFFICIENCY OF TRADING POST EQUILIBRIUM WITH COSTLY MEDIA OF EXCHANGE; AN ESSENTIAL TRADING POST ECONOMY

As in Hahn's (1973) and Starrett's (1973) analysis of a sequence economy, when the multi-faceted structure of the budget constraint in the trading post economy significantly affects the real allocation of resources, the resulting allocation is Pareto inefficient. This occurs because real resources spent or reallocated in fulfillment of the administrative requirement of budget constraints represent a waste. The expenditure or reallocation is administratively required but technically unnecessary.

### 4.1   Example: An Essential Trading Post Economy; Pareto-inefficient Allocation in Trading Post Equilibrium

The following example simply follows the format of the previous example, except that there is no costless medium of exchange. The result is a non-Walrasian Pareto-inefficient allocation. The mechanism of inefficiency is transparent. Transactions will use the medium of exchange and incur the cost of doing so. The cost is a wasted resource; it is administratively required but fulfills no technical function. Let the population $H$ and $H$'s endowments and preferences be as described in Section 3.1. There are $\frac{1}{2}N(N-1)$ firms denoted $\{i,j\}, j > i, i,j = 1, 2, \ldots, N$. The transaction technology of $\{i,j\}, i \neq 1$ is $Y^{\{i,j\}} \equiv \{(y,x)|$ for $k = i,j$, $0 \geq y_k \geq -0.8x_k$; for $k \neq i,j, y_k = x_k = 0\}$. For $\{i,j\}, i = 1, Y^{\{i,j\}} \equiv \{(y,x)|$ for $k = 1, y_1 = -x_1$, for $j \neq 1, 0 \geq y_1 + y_j \geq -0.9x_1 - 0.8x_j$; for $k \neq i,j$, $y_k = x_k = 0\}$. That is, for each pair of goods there is a distinct trading post firm $\{i,j\}$ and there is no arbitrage by firms between posts. Trade in all goods except good 1 experiences a 20 percent loss of each good in the trading process; trading two goods incurs two 20 percent losses, 20 percent of each. Trade in good 1 with any other good $j$ experiences a 30 percent loss in good $j$ (a 10 percent saving compared to using any good other than 1 as medium of exchange, hence the desirability of trading through good 1 if a medium of exchange is to be used).

The resulting equilibrium prices, using the notation of Chapter 11, for

$$i, j \neq 1 \text{ are } (\alpha_i^{\{i,j\}}, \beta_j^{\{i,j\}}) = \left(\frac{5}{8}, \frac{3}{8}\right).$$

For $i = 1, j \neq 2$ we have, $(\alpha_1^{\{1,j\}}, \beta_j^{\{1,j\}}) = \left(\frac{1}{2}, \frac{1}{2}\right), (\alpha_j^{\{1,j\}}, \beta_1^{\{1,j\}}) = \left(\frac{10}{17}, \frac{7}{17}\right).$

For $\{1,2\}$ we have $(\alpha_1^{\{1,2\}}, \beta_2^{\{1,j\}}) = \left(\frac{1}{2}, \frac{1}{2}\right), (\alpha_2^{\{1,2\}}, \beta_1^{\{1,j\}}) = \left(\frac{10}{17}, \frac{7}{17}\right).$

The trade flows for

$$h = 2, 3, \ldots, N-1, \text{ are } (x_h^{h\{h,1\}}, y_1^{h\{h,1\}}) = (-1, 1),$$

$$(x_1^{h\{1,h+1\}}, y_{h+1}^{h\{1,h+1\}}) = (-1, 0.7).$$

For $h = N, (x_N^{N\{1,N\}}, y_1^{N\{1,N\}}) = (-1, 0.7).$

For $h = 1, (x_1^{1\{1,2\}}, y_2^{1\{1,2\}}) = (-1, 0.7).$

That is, direct trade of most goods $i$ for $j$ is prohibitively expensive, losing 40 percent of the goods in the transaction process. This reflects the absence of double coincidence of wants. A typical household directly trading good $h$ for good $h + 1$ necessarily incurs transaction costs on both sides of the bargain. Indirect trade, through good 1, is more attractive since good 1 itself carries lower transaction costs. The typical pattern of trade then is that household $h$ sells endowment, good $h$, for good 1, then sells good 1 for the desired good, $h + 1$. In the process, only 30 percent of good $h + 1$ is lost to transaction costs.

In this example all trade goes through good 1, and for $N - 1$ out of $N$ traders good 1 is a medium of exchange. The allocation is not, however, Pareto efficient. Some of the resources used in the transaction process, 20 percent of gross endowment, is technically necessary to the reallocation. It is not wasted. But the transaction costs associated merely with fulfilling the pairwise trading post budget constraint, 10 percent of total endowment, is administratively necessary but not technically necessary. It is a waste. The equilibrium allocation represents the outcome in an essential trading post economy. It is not Pareto efficient.

Is the trading post equilibrium a Walrasian equilibrium? Individual agent trading behavior in the trading post model differs from Walrasian behavior (for example, in Foley, 1970) since it includes active use of a medium of exchange, good 1. Those trades net out to a loss. The resulting resource allocation is inconsistent with Walrasian equilibrium. In a Foley economy (Arrow–Debreu with transaction costs) the allocation cannot be supported by Walrasian equilibrium prices and it is Pareto inefficient. This trading post economy equilibrium is essential.

## 5  ECONOMIES NOT USING MEDIA OF EXCHANGE: DOUBLE COINCIDENCE OF WANTS AND INACTIVE TRADE

Economies with full double coincidence of wants and linear transaction costs will typically not use media of exchange in trading post equilibrium. Supplies are directly exchanged for demands.[2]

Alternatively, the economy may not use media of exchange simply because trade is unattractive. There are two obvious cases: a Pareto-efficient endowment and prohibitive transaction costs.

### 5.1  Full Double Coincidence of Wants with Linear Transaction Costs

Consider the following economy with full double coincidence of wants. Let $N \geq 2$ be an even integer. Let $H \equiv \{h = 1, 2, \ldots, N\}$ where $r_h^h = 100$ and where for $h$ odd $u^h(c^h) = 20c_{h+1}^h + \Sigma_{n \neq h+1, n=1}^N c_n^h$, and for $h$ even, $u^h(c^h) = 20c_{h-1}^h + \Sigma_{n \neq h-1, n=1}^N c_n^h$. There are $N$ households named $h = 1, 2, \ldots, N$; each endowed with 100 units of good $h$ and the odd numbered households strongly preferring good $h + 1$, the even numbered households strongly preferring good $h - 1$. Direct trade with the neighbor is the obvious policy. This will be true even if there is a low transaction cost instrument available, so long as direct trade is no more costly than indirect trade through the low transaction cost instrument.

Assume a population of firms and transaction technologies the same as in Section 4.1.

The resulting equilibrium prices, for

$$i, j \neq 1 \text{ are } (\alpha_i^{\{i,j\}}, \beta_j^{\{i,j\}}) = \left(\frac{5}{9}, \frac{4}{9}\right).$$

For $\{1, 2\}$ we have $(\alpha_1^{\{1,2\}}, \beta_2^{\{1,2\}}) = \left(\frac{10}{17}, \frac{7}{17}\right)$, $(\alpha_2^{\{1,2\}}, \beta_1^{\{1,2\}}) = \left(\frac{1}{2}, \frac{1}{2}\right)$.

The trade flows for $h$ odd, $h \neq 1, 2$ are

$$(x_h^{h\{h,h+1\}}, y_{h+1}^{h\{h,h+1\}}) = (-1, 0.8), \ (x_{h+1}^{h\{h,h+1\}}, y_h^{h\{h,h+1\}}) = (0, 0).$$

For $h = $ even, $(x_h^{h\{h,h-1\}}, y_{h-1}^{h\{h,h-1\}}) = (-1, 0.8), \ (x_{h-1}^{h\{h,h-1\}}, y_h^{h\{h,h-1\}}) = (0, 0)$.

For $h = 1, 2, (x_1^{1\{1,2\}}, y_2^{1\{1,2\}}) = (-1, 0.7), (x_2^{1\{1,2\}}, y_1^{1\{1,2\}}) = (0, 0), (x_1^{2\{1,2\}}, y_2^{2\{1,2\}}) = (0, 0), (y_1^{2\{1,2\}}, x_2^{2\{1,2\}}) = (1, -1)$.

All of the trade flows in this allocation are direct trade. There is no trade in media of exchange. This reflects the endowment, demand, and transaction cost structure: there is a double coincidence of wants, so there is little incentive to trade indirectly, and no transaction cost advantage to indirect trade. Thus, the example generates a trading post equilibrium without use of a medium of exchange. The trading structure and resulting allocation are Pareto efficient, and constitute a Walrasian equilibrium (allowing for transaction costs). The trading post economy is inessential. That is, the trade flows and resulting allocations would be the same – allowing for similar transaction technology – in a unified (Foley, 1970) trading setting.

## 5.2 Inactive Trade: Pareto-efficient Endowment

In an economy where there is no need for trade, there is no use for media of exchange. If the endowment is Pareto efficient, there will be no use of media of exchange in a trading post equilibrium.

### 5.3   Inactive Trade: Prohibitive Transaction Costs

A far more interesting reason for a nil demand for media of exchange is overwhelming transaction costs. Costs high enough to discourage all trade will eliminate the demand for media of exchange as well.

Assume household population, tastes and endowments, the same as in Section 3.1.

There are $\frac{1}{2}N(N-1)$ firms denoted $\{i,j\}, j > i, i, j = 1, 2, \ldots, N$. The transaction technology of $\{i,j\}$, all $i,j$, is $Y^{\{i,j\}} \equiv \{(y,x) | \text{for } k = i,j, 0 \geq y_k \geq -0.1x_k; \text{for } k \neq i,j, y_k = x_k = 0\}$. That is, for each pair of goods there is a distinct trading post firm $\{i, j\}$ and there is no arbitrage by firms between posts. Trade in all goods experiences a 90 percent loss in the trading process. A pair of trades using an intermediary good compounds the loss: 99 percent loss in two successive trades.

The resulting equilibrium prices, for

$$i, j \text{ are } (\alpha_i^{\{i,j\}}, \beta_j^{\{i,j\}}) = \left(\frac{99}{100}, \frac{1}{100}\right).$$

The endowment is the equilibrium allocation. No household wishes to trade at a discount of 99 percent — but this is just break-even for the firms considering the oppressive transaction technology. The allocation is non-Walrasian and is far from Pareto efficient — one-step rearrangements for each good would be a grand Pareto improvement, even incurring 90 percent transaction costs. But that calculation ignores the 90 percent transaction cost on payment of *quid pro quo*, necessarily incurred in a trading post equilibrium. This calculation reflects the dual problems of transaction costs and absence of double coincidence of wants — if there were a better match of suppliers with demanders even 90 percent transaction costs could be borne and mutually beneficial trades undertaken. But the absence of double coincidence of wants means that each trade undertaken benefits directly only one side. Two trades and two sets of transaction costs must be incurred in the trading post economy, and transaction costs then swamp the gains from trade.

## 6   CONCLUSION

Trading post equilibria are Pareto efficient when they are simply the elaboration of an underlying Walrasian equilibrium, an inessential trading post economy (see also Hahn, 1973). However, the multiplicity of separate budget constraints and the additional transaction costs incurred or avoided may skew the allocation and pricing (an essential trading post equilibrium). Then the equilibrium cannot be supported by a Walrasian price structure and the allocation will be Pareto inefficient (see also Starrett, 1973).

The price system is informative not only about scarcity and desirability. It also prices liquidity. Transaction costs generate a spread between bid and ask prices at each trading post. The bid—ask spread tells firms and households which goods are liquid, easily traded without significant loss of value, and which are illiquid, unsuitable as carriers of value between trades (Menger, 1892). The multiplicity of budget constraints creates the demand for liquidity; the bid—ask spreads signal its supply. When liquidity is too expensive (section 5.3), media of exchange will not be used. When liquidity is inexpensive and helpful in achieving a Pareto-improving allocation (example 3.1), media of exchange will be actively traded in equilibrium. The trading post model endogenously generates a designation and a flow of commodity money(s). The existence of (commodity) money and the monetary structure of trade is an outcome of the general economic equilibrium. Money is not a separate assumption; it is a result of the equilibrium allocation.

## NOTES

1. This chapter follows the approach of Starr (2008b).
2. Exceptions to this generalization occur where multiple trades through a medium of exchange incur a lower cost than a single direct trade. That reflects some cost associated with the interaction between the goods traded directly (for example, gasoline and matches) or economies of scale in a high-volume market with a common medium of exchange, as in Chapter 6.

# 13.   Alternative models

Monetary general equilibrium models include sequence economy models, overlapping generations models, and random matching models. Partial equilibrium models include models of the demand for money. Sequence economy models and money demand models emphasize the role of transaction costs, as does the trading post model. The general equilibrium models emphasize the sequential character of transactions – and hence the need for a carrier of value between transactions.

## 1   SEQUENCE ECONOMY

The approach closest in Arrow–Debreu style general equilibrium theory to a model of money occurs in a sequence economy model. This model modifies the notion that all trade for all time takes place in a grand single trade. Instead, markets reopen over time at each of a sequence of dates. Then there is a budget constraint at each market date. This framework generates demand for a carrier of value between market dates and hence a monetary instrument. Essays in this genre include Hahn (1971, 1973), Starrett (1973), Kurz (1974), Heller (1974), and Heller and Starr (1976). The treatment typically includes transaction costs so that bid and ask prices (or shadow bid and ask prices when the transaction costs are internalized to the transactors) may differ.

Several principal results then follow. There is a demand for 'money' or a commodity money carrier of value across time. In the case of set-up (nonconvex) transaction costs, the transaction cost structure may lead to inventory holding, both of real goods and of money.

The multiplicity of budget constraints may require (otherwise redundant) transactions to fulfill budgets at a sequence of dates, generating transaction costs or reallocations needed to fulfill budget constraints not required for desirable reallocation. Any resources used merely to fulfill budget constraints represent a deadweight loss. An intertemporal reallocation undertaken for transaction cost or budget balance reasons rather than to fulfill desired demands or supplies may represent an efficiency loss. Thus, a general equilibrium allocation of a sequence economy may not be Pareto efficient, contrary to the first fundamental theorem of welfare economics. This reflects that the wedge between bid and ask prices may generate a misallocation, if transactions incurring transaction costs are undertaken for purposes of budget balance.

However, if there is a zero transaction cost intertemporal carrier of value, 'money', the situation is reversed. All budget-balancing transactions are undertaken in the zero transaction cost money, incurring no unnecessary resource costs. Then the sequence economy equilibrium allocation is Pareto efficient (Starrett, 1973; Starr, 1978).

## 2 DEMAND FOR MONEY

A recurrent theme in pure and applied monetary economics is the notion of demand for money. Since money is held as a stock, its demand represents the quantity that firms and households will willingly hold over time. Typically, this quantity is thought to depend on prevailing interest rates (part of the opportunity cost of holding 'idle' money balances), trading volume, income, and uncertainty. The demand for money is certainly of policy interest since it is a significant parameter of monetary policy, affecting interest rates and − depending on the model and analysis − inflation rates and the value of nominal GDP.

There is a tradition in monetary theory to treat the demand for money as a stock in a distinctive fashion, differing from other household or firm demands. Thus Hicks (1935, p. 5) writes,

> The critical question arises when we look for an explanation of the preference for holding money rather than capital goods. For capital goods will ordinarily yield a positive rate of return which money does not. What has to be explained is the decision to hold assets in the form of barren money, rather than of interest- or profit-yielding securities . . .
> This, as I see it, is really the central issue in the pure theory of money . . .
> The most obvious sort of friction, and undoubtedly one of the most important, is the cost of transferring assets from one form to another.

Thus Hicks sets up the case for the Baumol (1952) and Tobin (1956) transaction cost-based inventory models of money holding. Fine, brilliantly simple models. But the notion that this family of issues is peculiar to money is mistaken. Households and firms hold many inventories, all arising from roughly the same foundations: nonconvex transaction costs. There is food in the refrigerator, in the freezer, and in the pantry; there are clothes in the closet and in the dresser; cars in the garage; an owner-occupied house. These are all inventories designed to be used, their quantity and depletion depending on interest rates, income, and transaction costs. There is nothing peculiar about the inventory of money. The demand for money as a stock requires no more complex theory than the demand for a stock of gasoline in the car's fuel tank or of a stock of clothing in the closet. That is the generality with which inventories are treated in Kurz (1974) and in the monetary model of Heller and Starr (1976).

## 3 OVERLAPPING GENERATIONS

The overlapping generations model traces its origins to Allais (1947) and Samuelson (1958). Its focus as a model of a monetary economy was most forcefully articulated by Wallace (1980). The abundance of that literature is far too numerous to cite. It has been an immensely fruitful model with a vast literature. The emphasis in the model is money as a store of value, an intertemporal asset allowing the reallocation of purchasing power over time. The underlying economic concept is that differing birth cohorts in the population will wish to trade with their successors but will possess nothing the latter values (think of the unproductive retired old seeking goods or services from the productive young). If the elders have money (acquired in their youth) and the young desire it (to provide for their own futures), then there are mutually beneficial monetary trades to be undertaken. The difficulty of finding a double coincidence of wants across generations creates the overlapping generations friction, which then accounts for the role of money.

Fiat money in this model is unbacked, a bubble whose positive price at any time is sustained by the expectation of a positive price in the future. Hence the model typically requires an infinite horizon. There is in addition a family of far less interesting nonmonetary equilibria. If the price of fiat money is zero, that is an equilibrium too. Then the model results in a nonmonetary equilibrium.

In order for money − at a positive price − to be willingly held, there must be no intertemporal asset with a higher yield. Thus typically the overlapping generations monetary model will not include productive capital or productive land. Tobin (1980), in his critique, notes that this model of money makes the frequency of monetary transaction once a generation, whereas in his view the frequency of transaction in actual economies is several orders of magnitude faster; indeed in the financial sector, several times a day.

# 4  RANDOM MATCHING

Random matching models — there have been papers far too numerous to cite here, the original is Kiyotaki and Wright (1993) — assume the existence of a fiat money. Trade is characterized as occurring in pairwise meetings between individuals. The issue is the classic question of double coincidence of wants. If two agents meet and there is a match of one's demand with the other's supply but not vice versa then the exchange of fiat money bridges the gap. This class of models has proved rich and fruitful.

Fiat money in this model is unbacked, a bubble whose positive price at any time is sustained by the expectation of a positive price in the future. Hence the model typically requires an infinite horizon. There is in addition a family of far less interesting nonmonetary equilibria. If the price of fiat money is zero, that is an equilibrium too. Then the model results in a nonmonetary equilibrium.

There is an implication that distinguishes the random matching model from the trading post model with scale economies in transaction costs (Chapter 6). Consider the rare event where two traders meet with mutually complementary demands and supplies (a double coincidence of wants). In the random matching model they exchange goods directly, without use of fiat money. This is certainly consistent with Jevons (1875). It is contrary to Clower (1967, p. 5), who writes 'Money buys goods; goods buy money. Goods do not buy goods'. But in the trading post model with scale economies in transaction cost (Chapter 6), even in the presence of double coincidence of wants, trade is monetary. This is consistent with the examples of auto workers buying cars with money, supermarket employees buying food with money, university faculty paying their children's tuition with money. Hence there is an implication that distinguishes between the models and may allow a choice of which is the more applicable.

# 14.  Conclusion and a research agenda

The examples of Chapters 3 through 8 present answers to the four puzzles set at the outset of this volume. But they are examples, not general results. A remaining research agenda includes general results emphasizing scale economy in transaction cost and network externality; elaboration of the sequence economy model; insertion of fiscal and transaction cost structure in the overlapping generations and random matching model; generalizing sufficient conditions for convergence to monetary equilibrium; and macroeconomics of the trading post model.

## 1   THE CHALLENGE AND RESULTS

The challenge of monetary economics to microeconomic theory was posed in Chapter 1. Can the pure theory of markets account for money: (i) trade is monetary; (ii) money is locally unique; (iii) it is a government-issued inherently useless fiat instrument; and (iv) it is used even when direct barter trade could be successfully applied.

Hahn (1982) agreed that it was a great challenge; Tobin (1980) said it was not possible. Nevertheless, a full general equilibrium trading post model (Chapter 11) generates a well-defined role for media of exchange – perhaps too many and too diverse. More convincingly, the class of examples developed in Chapters 3 to 8 generates equilibria with precisely the characteristics (i)–(iv).

How does the trading post model do this? The first step is to break up the array of transactions into many separate trades each requiring payment for goods delivered. That generates the demand for a medium (or media) of exchange. How then can we account for the universality and uniqueness of the medium of exchange. There may simply be a unique lowest transaction cost instrument (Chapter 4). Alternatively, there may be scale economies in the transaction technology so that uniqueness is endogenously determined (Chapter 6) – though which of many possible media of exchange becomes the locally unique choice is indeterminate.

How then does government create and retain the monopoly[1] on media of exchange? First by issuing a low transaction cost instrument; next by creating its value by making it acceptable in payment of taxes; finally by being a big enough economic agent that it generates the scale economy to sustain the natural monopoly (Chapter 8).

And the final conundrum: when there are mutually beneficial direct commodity trades available (double coincidence of wants) why do they go through a market with money rather than direct exchange? Scale economies in transaction costs (Chapter 6).

So all of the observations (i)−(iv) can be treated in this class of examples. Should we be satisfied? No, because they are just examples. They are not general results (with the exception of Chapter 11). Nevertheless, they provide clues to our comprehension.

## 2  RESEARCH AGENDA

### 2.1  Pure Theory of Money as a Natural Monopoly: An Ambitious Project

If the examples of Chapters 3 through 8 do not satisfy a craving for general results, what would a satisfactory general explanation of points (i)−(iv) look like? There appear to be two families of scale economies at work; a successful treatment will handle both together. At the level of the full economy there is the natural monopoly or network externality issue. Everyone finds it most convenient − least costly − to use the monetary instrument that everyone else is using. For the individual there are two set-up costs: the cost of dealing with an incremental market (Chapter 10) and the inventory-based scale economy (Baumol, 1952 and Tobin, 1956), creating the demand for the common medium of exchange as a stock. At the level of the individual transactor (household or firm) concentrating on a single medium of exchange rather than several generates a scale economy.

Combining the network externality and individual transactor scale effects in a single general equilibrium treatment is a challenge. General equilibrium does not find it easy to deal with large scale economies. That is why Chapters 3−8 use examples rather than general results and use average cost pricing rather than marginal cost pricing. Scale economies at the level of the individual agent can be systematically treated (Arrow and Hahn, 1971; Heller and Starr, 1976). Dealing with natural monopoly in general equilibrium is a bigger challenge. A natural monopoly pricing at marginal cost has the usual marginal cost pricing problems (Ruggles, 1950). The monopoly will typically need some inframarginal source of revenue to cover its inframarginal costs (Brown et al., 1992). In the case of a money-issuing natural monopoly, that revenue source is evident: seigniorage.

Modeling, in satisfactory generality, endogenous money is a worthy project and part of the research agenda for the trading post model. Money should appear as a marginal cost pricing natural monopoly with scale economies at two levels: the monetary authority and the individual transactor.

### 2.2 Sequence Economy and the Demand for Money

The sequence economy treatments of Radner (1972), Hahn (1971, 1973), and Starrett (1973) present a starting point for an alternative model of money reflecting a long-established premise. They provide a traditional rationale for use of money, the store of value. Markets reopen over time and a low-cost carrier of value across time is needed to bridge the gap. Fully monetizing the sequence economy model is unfinished business from decades ago. Does it need a trading post structure? Probably not. The multiplicity of trading opportunities in the sequence economy structure with transaction costs should be sufficient to express a theory of money as the low-cost store of value.

The more interesting formulation will deal with many long-lived assets including land, capital, and fiduciary instruments such as stocks and bonds. Then the issues of rate of return dominance versus the liquidity of the monetary instrument can be directly treated in the investigation. Will the Starrett (1973) efficiency result be sustained in this setting?

Hicks (1935), Baumol (1952), and Tobin (1956) clearly stated the sufficient conditions for demand for money as a stock. It should be possible to sustain them well in this sequence economy model (Heller, 1974; Heller and Starr, 1976).

### 2.3 Overlapping Generations and Random Matching

Can the overlapping generations and random matching models usefully be augmented with a trading post structure? Probably not. The impediments to direct trade in those models are sufficient without augmentation to generate a use for money to facilitate exchange. They could, however, be usefully augmented by a transaction cost and fiscal structure.

Both models use an infinite horizon and expectations of positive value of money in the future to sustain its positive value in the present. And they assume a monopoly for money as the long-lived instrument. The alternative is to derive these qualities from more elementary assumptions. Positive value can come from acceptability in payment of taxes (Li and Wright, 1998). That approach includes the possibility of eliminating the demonetized equilibria where money's value is zero. Monopoly can come from natural monopoly, unlimited scale economy in transaction costs.

A transaction cost structure with scale economy in transaction costs can eliminate an anomaly in the random matching model. Typically in that model, in the rare instance when two traders randomly meet with complementary demands and supplies (double coincidence of wants), they trade directly without use of money. For a model that emphasizes the absence of double coincidence of wants as a rationale for the use of money, this treatment makes perfect sense. Nevertheless, it is at odds with general experience (supermarket staff pay cash for their food). Expanding the random matching model to include transaction costs with a scale economy would allow the matched traders to decide whether to trade in monetary terms, optimizing their transaction costs.

### 2.4   Convergence to Monetary Equilibrium

Chapter 7 presented the example of convergence to monetary equilibrium in a tâtonnement process. But that was just an example. Can we get more general results? It is difficult to see how pure theory can give us fully general results. The special cases of overwhelming transaction costs and of Pareto-efficient endowment are in no sense anomalous and will surely result in no monetary equilibrium. Best guess is that the greater generality will come through computational simulation (see Newhouse, 2004 and Hu et al., 2010).

### 2.5   Macroeconomics of the Trading Post Monetary Model

One of the principal uses of the theory of money is to develop a theory of macroeconomics and of monetary policy. Can the trading post model of money usefully contribute to this program? It is not obvious. For most issues, the answer is probably 'no'.

The trading post model has been used in this volume to provide a microeconomic foundation for the use of a unique, monopolistic, government-issued, fiduciary money, used itself − or its immediate substitutes (denominated in the same units) − for virtually all transactions. For further policy modeling, it is probably sufficient to use this conclusion as a starting point. The microeconomic foundations do not matter until they begin to crumble. High rates of inflation and market illiquidity may be modeled using the trading post model, demonstrating where the smoothly functioning monetary system may break down.


## 3   CONCLUSION

There are two cornerstones to the extension of the theory of value to the theory of money: multiple budget constraints and variation in transaction costs. The former gives rise to the need for a carrier of value between transactions. The latter creates the scope for rational choice among carriers of value. The trading post model with transaction costs is an example of successful application of these premises.

This study started with four virtually universal observations:

- Trade is monetary. One side of almost all transactions is the economy's common medium of exchange.
- Money is (locally) unique. Though each economy has a 'money' and the 'money' differs among economies, almost all the transactions in most places most of the time use a single common medium of exchange.
- 'Money' is government-issued fiat money, trading at a positive value though it conveys directly no utility or production.
- Even transactions displaying a double coincidence of wants are transacted with money.

As universal economic observations, these results should have universal explanations in price theory, the fundamental first principles of economics. Chapters 3−11 provide demonstrations that a few simple additional specifications of the Arrow−Debreu general equilibrium model of price theory are sufficient to fulfill this need:

- each firm and household engages in many transactions each requiring payment for goods delivered;
- the transaction process is costly (resource using) perhaps displaying economies of scale;
- government is a large economic agent, creating obligations to itself, and issuing liabilities acceptable for payment of those obligations.

These modifications are sufficient to conclude all four observations as results of a price-theoretic general equilibrium.

# NOTE

1. The notion of monopoly here is not literally that government is the only issuer of media of exchange – checking accounts and credit cards are obvious substitutes. The monopoly consists in those alternative issuers denominating their instruments in the same units as the government's 'money.'

# Bibliography

Alchian, A. (1977), 'Why money?', *Journal of Money, Credit, and Banking*, **9** (1), pt. 2, February, 133−40.

Allais, M. (1947), *Économie et intérêt*, Paris: Imprimerie Nationale.

Aristotle (350 BCE), *Politics*, Jowett translation.

Arrow, K.J. (1951), 'An extension of the basic theorems of classical welfare economics', in Proceedings of the Second Berkeley Symposium on Mathematical Statistics and Probability, ed. J. Neyman, Berkeley, CA: University of California Press, pp. 507−32.

Arrow, K.J. (1953), 'Le rôle des valeurs boursières pour la repartition la meilleure des risques', *Économetrie*, Paris: Centre National de la recherche scientifique, pp. 41−8.

Arrow, K.J. (1964), 'The role of securities in the optimal allocation of risk-bearing', *Review of Economic Studies*, **31**, 91−6. English translation of Arrow (1953).

Arrow, K.J. and G. Debreu (1954), 'Existence of an equilibrium for a competitive economy', *Econometrica*, **22** (3), July, 265−90.

Arrow, K.J. and F.H. Hahn (1971), *General Competitive Analysis*, San Francisco, CA: Holden-Day.

Banerjee, A.V. and E.S. Maskin (1996), 'A Walrasian theory of money and barter', *Quarterly Journal of Economics*, **111** (4), November, 955−1005.

Baumol, W.J. (1952), 'The transactions demand for cash: an inventory theoretic approach', *Quarterly Journal of Economics*, **66** (4), November, 545−56.

Brown, D., W.P. Heller and R.M. Starr (1992), 'Two-part marginal cost pricing equilibrium: existence and efficiency', *Journal of Economic Theory*, **57** (1), June, 52−72.

Clower, R. (1967), 'A reconsideration of the microfoundations of monetary theory', *Western Economic Journal*, **6**, 1−8.

Clower, R. (1995), 'On the origin of monetary exchange', *Economic Inquiry*, **33**, 525−36.

Debreu, G. (1959), *Theory of Value*, New York: John Wiley & Sons.

Einzig, P. (1966), *Primitive Money*, Oxford: Pergamon Press.

Ellis, Howard (1934), *German Monetary Theory, 1905−1933*, Cambridge, MA: Harvard University Press.

Foley, D.K. (1970), 'Economic equilibrium with costly marketing', *Journal of Economic Theory*, **2** (3), 276−91.

Grandmont, J.-M. (1977), 'Temporary general equilibrium theory', *Econometrica*, **45** (3), April, 535−72.

Green, J. and W.P. Heller (1981), 'Mathematical analysis and convexity with applications to economics', in K.J. Arrow and M. Intriligator (eds), *Handbook of Mathematical Economics*, Vol. 1, Amsterdam: North-Holland.

Hahn, F.H. (1971), 'Equilibrium with transaction costs', *Econometrica*, **39** (3), 417−39.

Hahn, F.H. (1973), 'On transaction costs, inessential sequence economies and money', *Review of Economic Studies*, **40** (4), October, 449−61.

Hahn, F.H. (1982), *Money and Inflation*, Oxford: Basil Blackwell.

Hahn, F.H. (1997), 'Fundamentals', *Revista Internazionale di Scienze Sociali*, **105**, April−June, 123−38.

Heller, W.P. (1974), 'The holding of money balances in general equilibrium', *Journal of Economic Theory*, **7**, 93−108.

Heller, W. and R. Starr (1976), 'Equilibrium with non-convex transaction costs: monetary and non-monetary economies', *Review of Economic Studies*, **43** (2), 195−215.

Hellwig, C. (2000), 'Money, intermediaries and cash-in-advance constraints', London School of Economics, July 27, pdf duplicated.

Hendricks, K., M. Piccione and G. Tan (1992), 'The economics of hubs: the case of monopoly', photocopy, Department of Economics, University of British Columbia.

Hicks, J.R. (1935), 'A suggestion for simplifying the theory of money', *Economica*, **2** (5), 1−19.

Howitt, P. (2005), 'Beyond search: fiat money in organized exchange', *International Economic Review*, **46**, May, 405−29.

Howitt, P. and R. Clower (2000), 'The emergence of economic organization', *Journal of Economic Behavior and Organization*, **41**, 55−84.

Hu, Xue, Yu-Jung Whang, and Qiaoxi Zhang (2010), 'Convergence to monetary equilibrium: computational simulation of a trading post economy with transaction costs', University of California San Diego, available at: http://escholarship.org/uc/item/7br348nj.

Iwai, K. (1996), 'The bootstrap theory of money: a search theoretic foundation for monetary economics', *Structural Change and Economic Dynamics*, **7**, 451−77.

Jevons, W.S. (1875 [1919]), *Money and the Mechanism of Exchange*, London: D. Appleton.

Jones, R.A. (1976), 'The origin and development of media of exchange', *Journal of Political Economy*, **84**, 757−75.

Kaulla, R. (1920), *Grundlagen des geldwerts*, Stuttgart, 1920. Passage translated in Howard S. Ellis, *German Monetary Theory: 1903–1933*, Cambridge, MA: Harvard University Press, 1934.

Kiyotaki, N. and R. Wright (1989), 'On money as a medium of exchange', *Journal of Political Economy*, **97**, 927–54.

Kiyotaki, N. and R. Wright (1993), 'A search-theoretic approach to monetary economics', *American Economic Review*, **83** (1), March, 63–77.

Knapp, G.F. (1905 [1923]), *Staatliche Theorie des Geldes*, 4th edn, Munich and Leipzig: Duncker & Humblot. Translated as *The State Theory of Money*, London: Macmillan, 1924.

Kurz, M. (1974), 'Equilibrium in a finite sequence of markets with transaction cost', *Econometrica*, **42** (1), 1–20.

Lerner, A.P. (1947), 'Money as a creature of the state', in Proceedings of the American Economic Association, Vol. 37, pp. 312–17.

Li, Y. and R. Wright (1998), 'Government transaction policy, media of exchange, and prices', *Journal of Economic Theory*, **81** (2), August, 290–313.

Marimon, R., E. McGrattan and T. Sargent (1990), 'Money as medium of exchange in an economy with artificially intelligent agents', *Journal of Economic Dynamics and Control*, **14**, 329–73.

Menger, C. (1892), 'On the origin of money', *Economic Journal*, **2**, 239–55, trans. Caroline A. Foley. Reprinted in R. Starr (ed.), *General Equilibrium Models of Monetary Economies*, San Diego, CA: Academic Press, 1989, pp. 67–82.

Newhouse, H. (2004), 'The emergence of commodity money as a medium of exchange', PhD dissertation, University of California, San Diego.

Ostroy, J.M. (1973), 'The informational efficiency of monetary exchange', *American Economic Review*, **63** (4), 597–610.

Ostroy, J. and R. Starr (1974), 'Money and the decentralization of exchange', *Econometrica*, **42**, 597–610.

Ostroy, J. and R. Starr (1990), 'The transactions role of money', in B. Friedman and F. Hahn (eds), *Handbook of Monetary Economics*, New York: Elsevier, North-Holland, pp. 3–62.

Radford, R.A. (1945), 'The economic organisation of a P.O.W. camp', *Economica*, New Series, **12** (48), November, 189–201.

Radner, R. (1972), 'Existence of equilibrium of plans, prices, and price expectations in a sequence of markets', *Econometrica*, **40** (2), March, 289–303.

Rajeev, M. (1999), 'Marketless set-up vs trading posts: a comparative analysis', *Annales d'Économie et de Statistique*, n. 53, January–March, 197–211.

Rey, H. (2001), 'International trade and currency exchange', *Review of Economic Studies*, **68** (2), April, 443−64.

Rogawski, J. and M. Shubik (1986), 'A strategic market game with transaction costs', *Mathematical Social Sciences*, **11** (2), 139−60.

Roscher, W. (1878), *Principles of Political Economy*, New York. First German edition 1854. Quoted in J. Schumpeter, *History of Economic Analysis*, New York: Oxford University Press, 1954.

Ruggles, N.D. (1950), 'Recent developments in the theory of marginal cost pricing', *Review of Economic Studies*, **17** (2), 107−26.

Samuelson, P. (1958), 'An exact consumption-loan model of interest with or without the social contrivance of money', *Journal of Political Economy*, **66** (6), 467−82.

Schumpeter, J.A. (1954), *History of Economic Analysis*, New York: Oxford University Press.

Shapley, L.S. and M. Shubik (1977), 'Trade using one commodity as means of payment', *Journal of Political Economy*, **85** (5), October, 937−68.

Shubik, M. (1973), 'Commodity money, oligopoly, credit and bankruptcy in a general equilibrium model', *Western Economic Journal*, **11**, March, 24−38.

Shubik, M. (1993), *The Theory of Money and Financial Institutions*, Cambridge, MA: MIT Press.

Smith, A. (1776), *An Inquiry into the Nature and Causes of the Wealth of Nations*, Volume I, Book II, Chap. II, London: W. Strahan & T. Cadell.

Starr, R.M. (1972), 'The structure of exchange in barter and monetary economics', *Quarterly Journal of Economics*, **86** (2), May, 290−302.

Starr, R.M. (1974), 'The price of money in a pure exchange monetary economy with taxation', *Econometrica*, **42**, 45−54.

Starr, R.M. (1978), 'Money in sequence economy: a correction', *Review of Economic Studies*, **45** (2), June, 391.

Starr, R.M. (1997), *General Equilibrium Theory: An Introduction*, New York: Cambridge University Press.

Starr, R. (2003), 'Why is there money? Endogenous derivation of "money" as the most liquid asset: a class of examples', *Economic Theory*, **21** (2−3), March, 455−74.

Starr, R. (2004), 'Existence and uniqueness of "money", in general equilibrium: natural monopoly in the most liquid asset', in C.D. Aliprantis, K.J. Arrow, P. Hammond, F. Kubler, H.-M. Wu and N.C. Yannelis (eds), *Assets, Beliefs, and Equilibria in Economic Dynamics*, Heidelberg: BertelsmanSpringer, pp. 269−302.

Starr, R. (2008a), 'Mengerian saleableness and commodity money in a Walrasian trading post example', *Economics Letters*, **100**, 35−8.

Starr, R. (2008b), 'Commodity money equilibrium in a convex trading post economy with transaction costs', *Journal of Mathematical Economics*, **44**, 1413–27.

Starr, R. (2010), 'The Jevons double coincidence condition and local uniqueness of money: an example', *Journal of Mathematical Economics*, **46**, 786–92.

Starr, R.M. and M.B. Stinchcombe (1992), 'Efficient transportation routing and natural monopoly in the airline industry: an economic analysis of hub–spoke and related systems', Working Paper, University of California, San Diego, May.

Starr, R.M. and M.B. Stinchcombe (1999), 'Exchange in a network of trading posts', in G. Chichilnisky (ed.), *Markets, Information, and Uncertainty: Essays in Economic Theory in Honor of Kenneth Arrow*, Cambridge: Cambridge University Press, pp. 216–34.

Starrett, D.A. (1973), 'Inefficiency and the demand for money in a sequence economy', *Review of Economic Studies*, **40** (4), 437–48.

Tobin, J. (1956), 'The interest-elasticity of transactions demand for cash', *Review of Economics and Statistics*, **38** (3), August, 241–47.

Tobin, J. (1959), *The Tobin Manuscript*, New Haven, CT: Yale University mimeo.

Tobin, J. (1961), 'Money, capital, and other stores of value', *American Economic Review*, **51** (2), 26–37.

Tobin, J. (1980), 'Discussion', in J. Kareken and N. Wallace, *Models of Monetary Economies*, Minneapolis, MN: Federal Reserve Bank of Minneapolis, pp. 83–90.

Tobin, J. with S. Golub (1998), *Money, Credit, and Capital*, Boston, MA: Irwin/McGraw-Hill.

Trejos, A. and R. Wright (1995), 'Search, bargaining, money and prices', *Journal of Political Economy*, **103** (1), 118–41.

Wallace, N. (1980), 'The overlapping generations model of fiat money', in J. Kareken and N. Wallace, *Models of Monetary Economies*, Minneapolis, MN: Federal Reserve Bank of Minneapolis, pp. 49–82.

Walras, L. (1874), *Elements of Pure Economics*, Jaffe translation (1954), Homewood, IL: Irwin.

Wicksell, K. (1898), *Geldzins und Güterpreise. Eine Untersuchung über die den Tauschwert des Geldes bestimmenden Ursachen*, Jena: Gustav Fischer. Translated as *Interest and Prices. A Study of the Causes Regulating the Value of Money*, London: Macmillan, 1936.

Young, H.P. (1998), *Individual Strategy and Social Structure: An Evolutionary Theory of Institutions*, Princeton, NJ: Princeton University Press.

# Index